# Reading Comprehension and Skills: Grade 1

W9-AVM-826

## Table of Contents

ISBN 978-1-60418-253-8

# Ready-to-Use Ideas and Activities

This book was developed to help students master the basic skills necessary to become competent readers. The stronger their foundation in reading basics, the faster and easier children will be able to advance to more challenging texts.

Mastering the skills covered within the activity pages of this book is paramount for successful reading comprehension. The activities at the beginning of the book aim to build and reinforce vocabulary, the foundation of reading comprehension. These activities lead to practice with more advanced comprehension skills such as categorizing and using context to understand words. Then, at the end of the book, students begin to practice answering comprehension questions about progressively longer stories.

All children learn at their own rate; therefore, use your judgment to introduce concepts to children when developmentally appropriate.

## Hands-On Learning

Hands-on learning reinforces the skills covered within the activity pages and improves students' potential for comprehension. One idea for a hands-on activity is to use the removable flash cards at the back of this book to play a game of bingo. To do this, make a copy of the bingo card on the next page for each student. Write the flash card words on the board and have students choose 24 of the words and write them in the empty spaces of their bingo cards in any order. When students have finished writing on their cards, gather the flash cards into a deck. Call out the words one at a time. Any student who has a word that you call out should make an X through the word on her card to cross it out. The student who crosses out five words in a row first (horizontally, vertically, or diagonally) wins the game by calling out, "Bingo!" To extend the game, you can continue playing until a student crosses out all of the words on his bingo card.

## Comprehension Checks and Discussion

In addition to the activities in this book, you can support reading comprehension growth when you read stories in the classroom. After a story—or part of a story—is read, ask your students questions to ensure and enhance reading comprehension. The first type of question you might ask is a factual question. A factual question includes question words such as *who, what, when, where, how,* and *why.* For example, *How old is the character?, Where does the character live?, What time was it when ?,* or any other question that has a clear answer. You might also ask open-ended questions. These types of questions do not have a clear answer. They are based on opinions about the story, not on facts. For example, an open-ended question might be, *Why do you think the character acted as he did?, How do you think the character felt about her actions or the actions of others?, What do you think the character will do next?,* or *What other ways could this story have ended?*

# Vocabulary Bingo

| | | | | |
|---|---|---|---|---|
| | | | | |
| | | | | |
| | | FREE | | |
| | | | | |
| | | | | |

Name _____

# First Letter

Look at each set of letters. Draw a line from the picture to the letter the picture begins with. Not every letter will have a match.

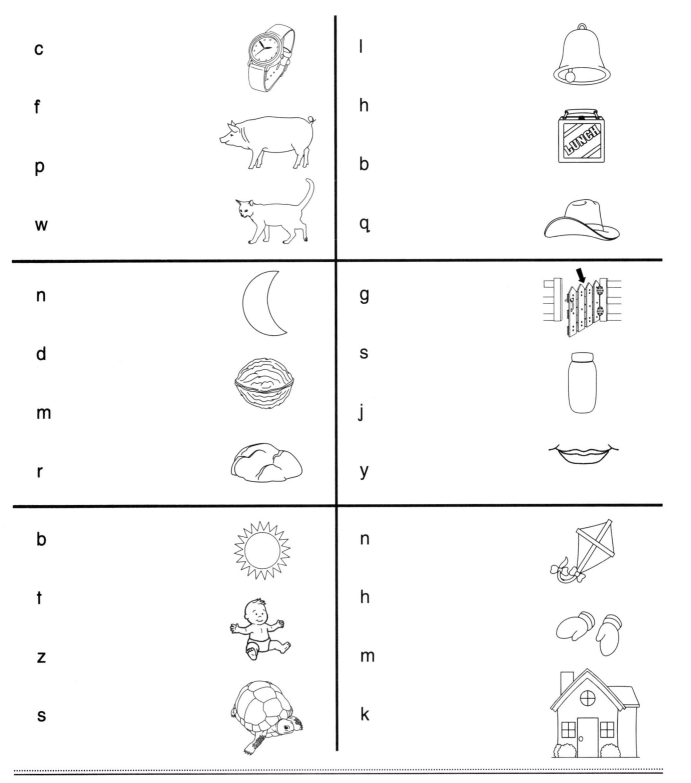

CD-104303 • © Carson-Dellosa

# First Letter

Look at each set of letters. Draw a line from the picture to the letter the picture begins with. Not every letter will have a match.

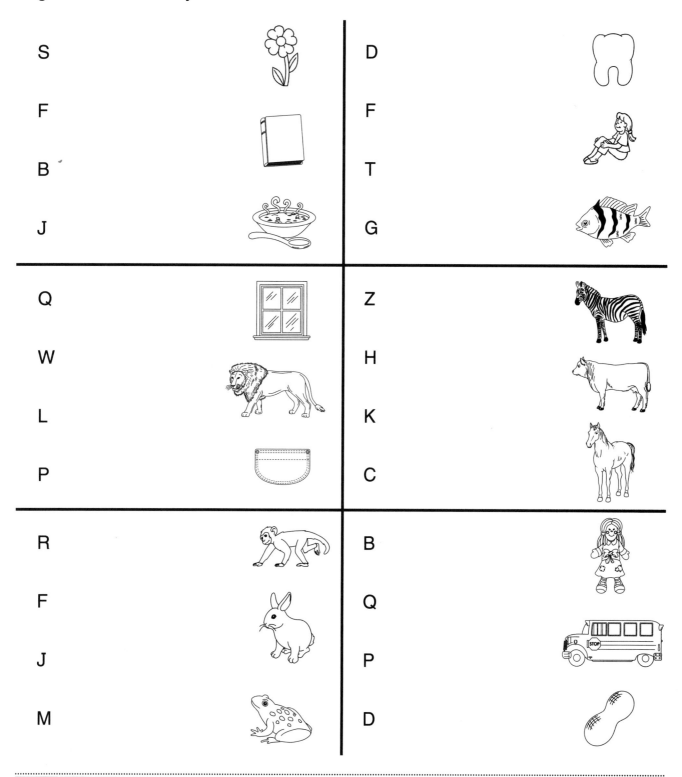

Name _____

# First Letter

Look at each letter. Circle the picture that begins with that letter.

Name _____

# First Letter

Look at each picture. Circle the letter that the picture begins with.

|  |  |  |
|---|---|---|
| p    l    r | d    n    s | z    f    c |
| g    n    q | h    y    s | k    l    j |
| B    R    T | V    F    X | P    Z    D |
| G    B    L | Y    K    N | R    F    M |

# Last Letter

Look at each picture. Draw a line to match each letter to the picture that ends with that letter. Not every letter will have a match.

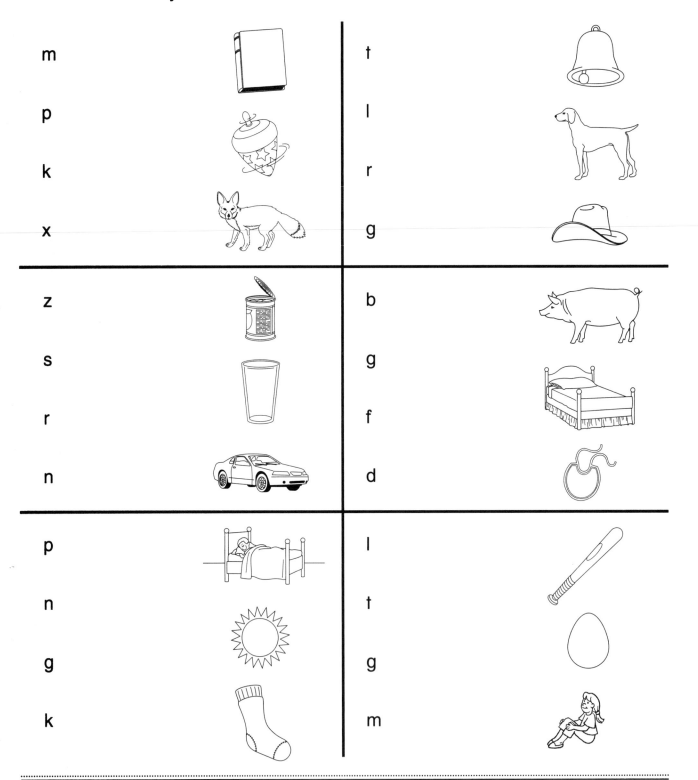

m

p

k

x

t

l

r

g

z

s

r

n

b

g

f

d

p

n

g

k

l

t

g

m

Name _____

# Last Letter

Look at each set of letters. Draw a line to match each letter to the picture that ends with that letter. Not every letter will have a match.

# Last Letter

Look at each letter. Circle the picture that ends with that letter.

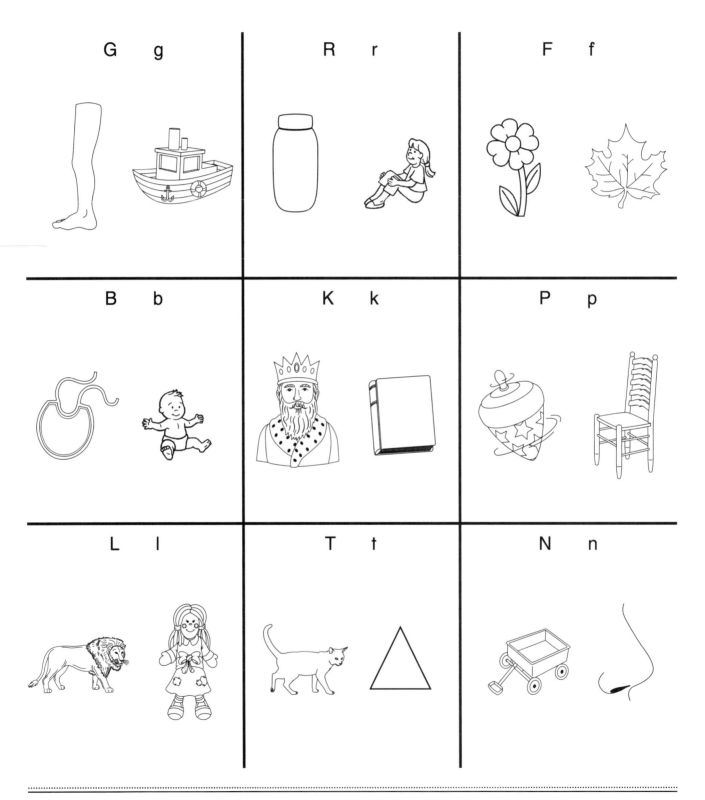

# Last Letter

Look at each picture. Circle the letter that the picture ends with.

|  |  |  |
|---|---|---|
| l    p    s | g    n    t | d    m    z |
| k    d    s | t    d    b | f    r    x |
| P    F    T | K    S    D | M    D    L |
| S    B    N | N    F    K | L    R    M |

# First and Last Letter

Look at each picture. Fill in the blanks to complete the word that names the picture.

| _____ i _____ | _____ ago _____ | _____ ir _____ |
| _____ el _____ | _____ o _____ | _____ ow _____ |
| _____ oa _____ | _____ ou _____ | _____ or _____ |

Name _____

# First and Last Letter

Look at each picture. Fill in the blanks to complete the word that names the picture.

_____ ea _____        _____ or _____        _____ oc _____

_____ ar _____        _____ oo _____        _____ e _____

_____ res _____        _____ u _____        _____ oo _____

Name _____

# -*s* Ending

Choose the correct word for each sentence. Write the word in the blank.

1. Julie _____ her dog.

   I _____ my cat.

   hug     hugs

2. Mary will _____ dinner.

   She _____ a pizza.

   cook     cooks

3. I _____ in my bed.

   Rover _____ on the floor.

   sleep     sleeps

4. Oscar _____ soup.

   I _____ salad.

   eat     eats

5. We will _____ fast.

   Lee _____ home.

   jog     jogs

6. The cake _____ good.

   I can _____ the soup.

   smell     smells

7. Kitty _____ to play.

   They _____ to read.

   like     likes

8. I _____ my milk.

   Mom _____ her tea.

   drink     drinks

Name _____

# -*s* Ending

Look at the pictures in each row. Choose the words that go with the picture and write the words in the blank.

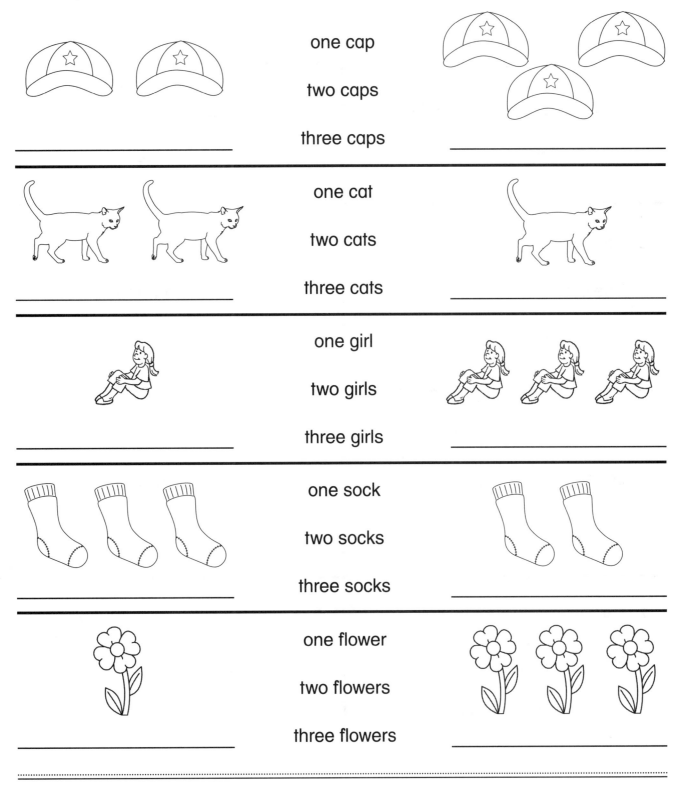

one cap

two caps

three caps

_____        _____

one cat

two cats

three cats

_____        _____

one girl

two girls

three girls

_____        _____

one sock

two socks

three socks

_____        _____

one flower

two flowers

three flowers

_____        _____

Name _____

# -es Ending

Choose the correct word for each sentence. Write the word in the blank.

1. My _____ is in a bowl.

   Dad _____ in the pond.

   fish      fishes

2. She _____ to school.

   They _____ to work.

   go      goes

3. Please _____ your step.

   The cat _____ for mice.

   watch      watches

4. Mom _____ our team.

   I _____ my little sister.

   coach      coaches

5. I will _____ the problem.

   Jean _____ her bike.

   fix      fixes

6. Tia _____ her cookie.

   I _____ sandwiches.

   eats      eat

7. I will _____ my hair.

   Peg _____ her hair often.

   brush      brushes

8. Sandy _____ the ball.

   Do not _____ a cold.

   catch      catches

# -*es* Ending

Look at each picture. Circle the word that matches the picture.

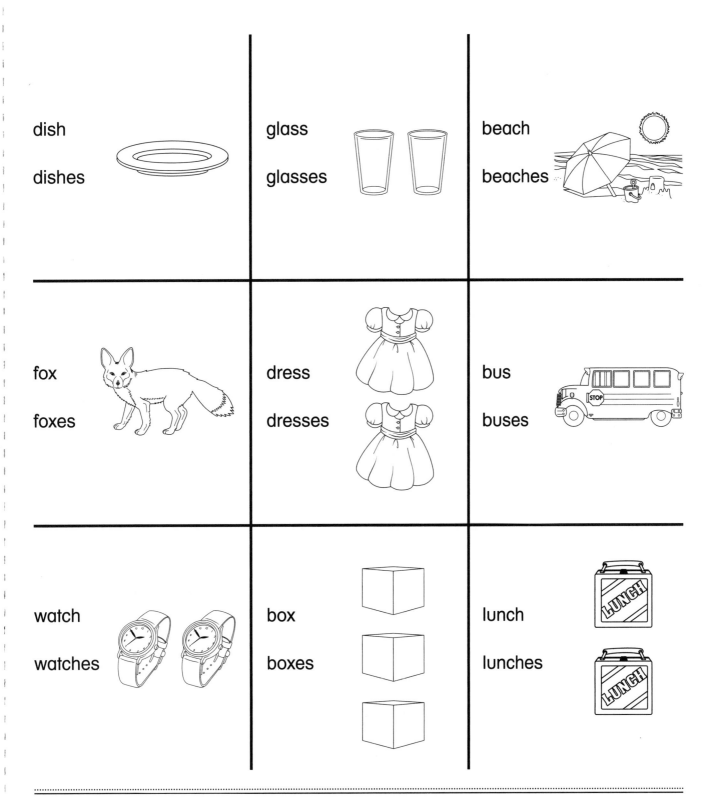

dish

dishes

glass

glasses

beach

beaches

fox

foxes

dress

dresses

bus

buses

watch

watches

box

boxes

lunch

lunches

Name _____

# -*s* or -*es* Ending

Look at the picture in each row. Circle the word that matches the picture.

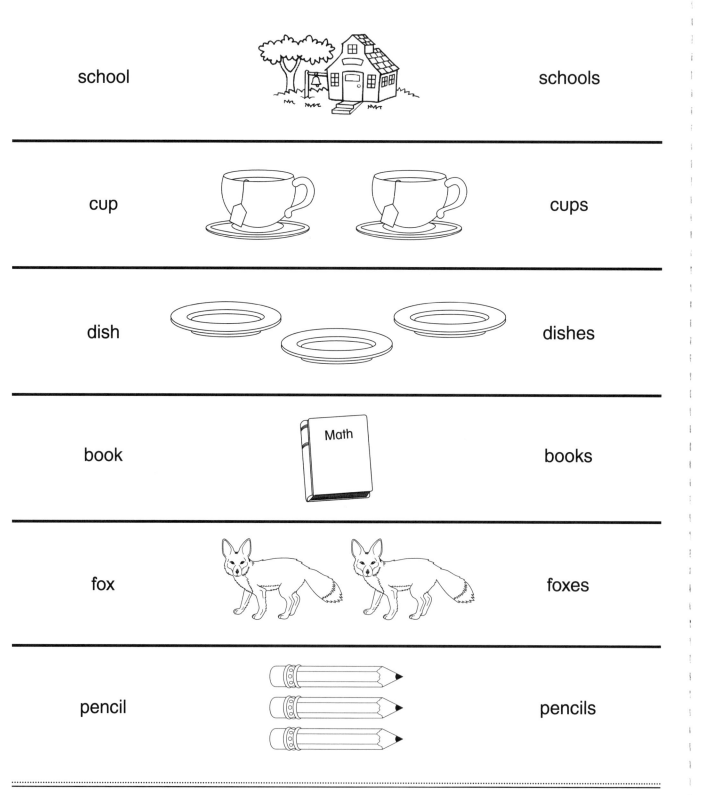

school                schools

cup                cups

dish                dishes

book                books

fox                foxes

pencil                pencils

# -*er* Ending

Read each sentence. Fill in the blank with the correct word.

1. I am _____ than my brother.          smart      smarter

2. He is a _____ man.          thin      thinner

3. Jan is _____ than her sister.          young      younger

4. Rain is _____ than sunshine.          sad      sadder

5. The sun is _____ like a ball.          round      rounder

6. Night is _____ than day.          dark      darker

7. My pencil is very _____.          sharp      sharper

8. The grass is _____.          green      greener

9. The teacher is _____ than his students.          old      older

10. The sun is _____ than the moon.          bright      brighter

# -ed Ending

Read each sentence. Fill in the blank with the correct word.

1. The rabbit _____ in the grass.          hop          hopped

2. I will _____ my room.          clean          cleaned

3. Mom _____ for a new car.          look          looked

4. We _____ when he told a joke.          laugh          laughed

5. Nan _____ her milk.          spill          spilled

6. Please _____ the right answer.          circle          circled

7. Dad _____ at the lake.          fish          fished

8. Mike _____ to school this morning.          walk          walked

9. I _____ the ball to her a minute ago.          roll          rolled

10. Kate _____ her car last week.          fix          fixed

Name _____

# -*er* or -*ed* Ending

Read each sentence. Fill in the blank with the correct word.

1. The barn is _____ than the house.          red          redder

2. Grandma _____ carefully onto the ladder.          step          stepped

3. The tree was as _____ as the child.          tall          taller

4. This box is _____ than that one.          light          lighter

5. She _____ the dog on the head.          pat          patted

6. I like to _____ to the store.          walk          walked

7. The _____ snake moves in the grass.          long          longer

8. Matt _____ off the high board.          jump          jumped

9. We want to _____ down the river.          row          rowed

10. The kitten is _____ than the cat.          small          smaller

Name _____

# -er or -ed Ending

Read each sentence. Fill in the blank with the correct word.

1. Please _____ your work.          finish          finished

2. Ms. Dove is my _____.          teach          teacher

3. The _____ stepped into the ring.          box          boxer

4. Pete is a good _____.          cook          cooked

5. We will _____ to play soccer.          learn          learned

6. Mary _____ down the sidewalk.          skip          skipped

7. I am a good _____.          read          reader

8. We _____ a farm.          own          owner

9. Please _____ to the next chair.          move          moved

10. My pony is very _____.          fast          faster

# Synonyms

For each sentence, read the list of words. Circle the word that means almost the same thing as the underlined word.

| | | | |
|---|---|---|---|
| 1. I was <u>glad</u> to finish the test. | happy | mad | warm |
| 2. Sue and Rick like to <u>talk</u>. | run | speak | swim |
| 3. You did a <u>nice</u> job. | bad | great | wide |
| 4. Fred's <u>boots</u> got wet in the rain. | hands | books | shoes |
| 5. Alice has three <u>children</u>. | kids | animals | friends |
| 6. Tom is <u>afraid</u> of dogs. | angry | scared | cats |
| 7. We used <u>glue</u> in art class. | paper | paint | paste |
| 8. Aunt Ellen has a <u>beautiful</u> house. | pretty | home | big |

# Synonyms

For each sentence, read the list of words. Circle the word that means almost the same thing as the underlined word.

| | | | |
|---|---|---|---|
| 1. Please <u>shut</u> the door. | open | close | window |
| 2. You can <u>fold</u> the paper in half. | bend | flower | pen |
| 3. Jo's <u>bag</u> is full of books. | bat | sack | table |
| 4. Dad will <u>bake</u> a cake. | cook | eat | cut |
| 5. I want a <u>small</u> lunch. | dinner | big | little |
| 6. A rabbit is <u>quick</u>. | fast | brown | quiet |
| 7. Dave will <u>begin</u> the song. | start | end | sing |
| 8. My <u>dad</u> won first place. | father | mom | game |

# Antonyms

Read each list of words. Circle the word that is the opposite of the first word.

| 1. **night** | sleep | day | sun |
| --- | --- | --- | --- |
| 2. **thick** | thin | white | wide |
| 3. **quick** | fast | quiet | slow |
| 4. **always** | never | time | short |
| 5. **sad** | happy | smile | blue |
| 6. **high** | tall | tree | low |
| 7. **hot** | warm | cold | ice |
| 8. **leave** | return | go | sleep |

# Antonyms

Read each list of words. Circle the word that is the opposite of the first word.

| 1. **quiet** | loud | soft | hard |
| 2. **good** | bad | nice | sad |
| 3. **new** | hot | old | quiet |
| 4. **yes** | not | no | maybe |
| 5. **right** | wrong | good | write |
| 6. **scream** | talk | cry | whisper |
| 7. **alike** | different | love | pair |
| 8. **sunny** | hot | rainy | summer |

Name _____

# What Is It?

Read each question. Circle the word that answers the question. Use the word in a sentence that answers the question.

1. What is small?            house            school            kitten

   _____

2. What is hard?            sock            milk            rock

   _____

3. What smells good?            socks            book            flower

   _____

4. What can you open?            rug            window            king

   _____

5. What shines at night?            moon            sun            bed

   _____

6. What lives in water?            fish            basketball            clown

   _____

# What Is It?

Read each question. Circle the word that answers the question. Use the word in a sentence that answers the question.

1. What can a horse do?    cook    race    whisper

_____

2. What can you cook?    soup    kitchen    shovel

_____

3. What do you sleep on?    table    basket    bed

_____

4. What has stripes?    zebra    lion    crown

_____

5. What tastes sweet?    cake    dish    meat

_____

6. What can you wear?    picnic    cat    clothes

_____

# What Am I?

Read the clues for each riddle. Circle the correct answer.

I am long.
I have a point.
I help you write.
What am I?

book        pencil

math        teacher

I can fly.
I have pretty wings.
I sip from flowers.
What am I?

chicken     grass

butterfly   horse

I am orange.
I am round.
I have a green stem.
What am I?

pumpkin    spoon

house      apple

I climb trees.
I make funny faces.
I hang by my tail.
What am I?

monkey     goat

dog        bird

I have two wheels.
I can go fast.
Children can ride me.
What am I?

car        bike

horse      truck

I am round.
I am full of air.
I float in the sky.
What am I?

coat       bone

ball       balloon

# What Am I?

Read the clues for each riddle. Circle the correct answer.

I am brown or gray.
I have a big tail.
I eat acorns.
What am I?

tree        shell

squirrel    cat

---

I am round.
I can be many colors.
I help you see.
What am I?

ears        eyes

nose        face

---

I have four legs.
I am made of wood or metal.
I belong at a table.
What am I?

chair       teacher

tree        bird

---

I am large.
I can swim.
I live in the sea.
What am I?

boat        goldfish

water       whale

---

I am soft.
I have sheets.
I help you rest.
What am I?

bed         jeans

floor       home

---

I am fluffy.
I live in the sky.
I can be white, gray, or black.
What am I?

sun         moon

cloud       drop

# What Does Not Belong?

Read each list of words. Circle the word that does not go with the others.

1. apple          orange          banana          glass

2. mother          father          elephant          son

3. five          clock          six          two

4. whale          shark          dolphin          swim

5. flower          bow          plant          seed

6. fork          spoon          knife          grass

7. hair          eyes          turtle          nose

8. read          finger          study          play

Name _____

# What Does Not Belong?

Read each list of words. Circle the word that does not go with the others.

1. pencil        crayon        paper        pen

2. mug        cup        glass        table

3. class        farm        school        teacher

4. sun        star        grass        moon

5. yellow        car        orange        blue

6. sit        stand        chair        lie

7. king        prince        queen        frog

8. coat        rose        pants        shirt

# Yes or No?

Read each sentence. Decide whether it is true. Circle yes or no.

Yes  No

A kitten can fly.

| | | |
|---|---|---|
| A school can jump. | Yes | No |
| Pigs can eat. | Yes | No |
| All horses are white. | Yes | No |
| Kids can walk down the street. | Yes | No |
| All books are short. | Yes | No |
| A fox can speak. | Yes | No |
| You can roll a ball. | Yes | No |
| Boys can sing songs. | Yes | No |
| A snail can run. | Yes | No |
| All rabbits are big. | Yes | No |
| A plane is faster than a car. | Yes | No |
| The moon is green. | Yes | No |

# Yes or No?

Read each sentence. Decide whether it is true. Circle yes or no.

Yes                                                No

A girl can go to school.

| | | |
|---|---|---|
| The sun gives us light. | Yes | No |
| All puppies are huge. | Yes | No |
| Cars can go to work. | Yes | No |
| Children can do math. | Yes | No |

| | | |
|---|---|---|
| Teams always win. | Yes | No |
| Pencils can be sharp. | Yes | No |
| Fish can read. | Yes | No |
| All houses are blue. | Yes | No |

| | | |
|---|---|---|
| A door can be made of wood. | Yes | No |
| All crayons are red. | Yes | No |
| A frog can hop. | Yes | No |
| A snake can walk. | Yes | No |

# Rhymes

Read each list of words. Circle the words that rhyme with the first word.

| 1. **jig** | jug | fig | pig | jog | big |
|---|---|---|---|---|---|
| 2. **sap** | sip | map | tap | stop | trap |
| 3. **vine** | fine | tree | line | pine | vet |
| 4. **ball** | bell | wall | tall | bowl | hall |
| 5. **hot** | tot | cold | warm | cot | not |
| 6. **pail** | pill | nail | sail | pile | tail |
| 7. **old** | young | fold | cold | age | sold |
| 8. **pat** | sat | that | get | pet | cat |

Name _____

# Rhymes

Read each list of words. Circle the words that rhyme with the first word.

| 1. **glass** | pass | gloss | milk | mass | class |
| 2. **most** | post | toast | tall | bed | host |
| 3. **neat** | messy | meat | clean | beat | heat |
| 4. **tan** | can | white | ran | plan | sun |
| 5. **stool** | chair | cool | pool | sit | fool |
| 6. **pen** | hen | den | pencil | paper | ten |
| 7. **gate** | late | slate | door | skate | lock |
| 8. **bad** | dad | sad | beam | grade | lad |

# Multiple Meanings

Look at the pictures. Draw a line to match each picture with the correct sentence.

My brother is in a band.

True friends band together.

---

A guard stands at the door.

I guard my cake.

---

Amy has a pretty ring.

We ring the bell on Friday.

---

Please get the mail.

Leah needs to mail a letter.

---

Dad writes with a pen.

The pig was in a pen.

# Find the Right Word

Read each sentence. Fill in the blank with the correct word to complete the sentence.

1. Jerry _____ me a new pencil.                give        gave

2. We _____ our toy boat.                       sailed      sails

3. Mom and Dad _____ to the store.              goes        went

4. Penny _____ an old friend.                   meet        met

5. Ali _____ the eagle fly above her.           saw         seen

6. Gina _____ a good student.                   become      became

7. I _____ a baby sister.                       has         have

8. We _____ you for coming.                     thank       thanks

9. A plane _____ high.                          fly         flies

10. The sun _____ shining.                      were        was

# Find the Right Word

Read each sentence. Fill in the blank with the correct word to complete the sentence.

1. Ray _____ well.                     listen        listens

2. She _____ to play tag.              loves         love

3. Sheri can _____ ten laps.           swam          swim

4. Jen _____ the circus show.          watch         watched

5. He _____ the wet shirt.             dried         dry

6. My brother _____ in the park.       played        play

7. I _____ the last cookie.            takes         took

8. Phil _____ late.                     am            was

9. Monkeys _____ me laugh.              make          makes

10. Trina _____ a blue ring.            have          has

# Find the Right Word

Read each sentence. Fill in the blank with the correct word to complete the sentence.

I. Mom _____ her gold necklace.          wear          wore

___

2. Pam _____ my best friend.          are          is

___

3. We _____ to draw.          like          likes

___

4. The dog _____ to her.          run          ran

___

5. Mr. Ang _____ a story.          told          tell

___

6. I _____ Dad good-bye.          hugs          hugged

___

7. That puppy _____ a lot.          eat          eats

___

8. The road _____ bumpy.          was          were

___

9. Her car _____ too slowly.          goes          go

___

10. Mark _____ his lunch.          want          wants

# Find the Right Word

Read each sentence. Fill in the blank with the correct word to complete the sentence.

I. My friend read ten _____.          books          book

2. Her _____ played with her.          mothers          mother

3. Ten _____ rode in the car.          clown          clowns

4. One _____ will win.          teams          team

5. Paul likes to tell _____.          joke          jokes

6. I have two _____ in my pocket.          dime          dimes

7. Harry has six _____.          parrots          parrot

8. Their family has two _____.          van          vans

9. Our town has one _____.          pool          pools

10. Todd ate three _____ of pie.          pieces          piece

Read the sentences under the picture. Fill in the blanks.

# Pat

The girl is Pat.
She is in first grade.

1. The girl is _____.

2. The _____ is Pat.

3. _____ girl is Pat.

4. She is in _____ grade.

5. _____ is in first grade.

6. The _____ is _____.

7. _____ is in _____ grade.

CD-104303 • © Carson-Dellosa

Name _____

Read the sentences under the picture. Fill in the blanks.

# Tad

I have a dog.
His name is Tad.

1. I have a _____.

2. _____ have a dog.

3. _____ name is Tad.

4. His name is _____.

5. His _____ is Tad.

6. _____ have a _____.

7. His _____ is _____.

Name _____

Read the sentences under the picture. Fill in the blanks.

# Jim

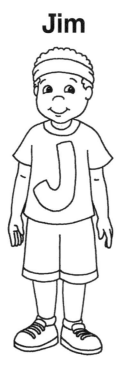

Jim is my pal.
He likes to run.

1. Jim is my _____.

2. _____ is my pal.

3. Jim is _____ pal.

4. He likes to _____.

5. _____ likes to run.

6. _____ is my _____.

7. _____ likes to _____.

Name _____

Read the sentences under the picture. Fill in the blanks.

# Ms. Fry

Ms. Fry teaches art.
She is a fun teacher.

1. Ms. Fry teaches _____.

2. Ms. _____ teaches art.

3. She is a _____ teacher.

4. _____ is a fun teacher.

5. She is a fun _____.

6. Ms. _____ teaches _____.

7. _____ is a _____ teacher.

Name _____

Read the sentences under the picture. Fill in the blanks.

# My School

I like my school.
I ride a bus to school.

1. I like my _____.

2. I _____ my school.

3. I like _____ school.

4. I _____ a bus to school.

5. I ride a _____ to school.

6. I _____ my _____.

7. I _____ a _____ to school.

Name _____

Read the sentences under the picture. Fill in the blanks.

# My Dad

My dad packs my lunch.
He waves to me.

1. My _____ packs my lunch.

2. My dad packs my _____.

3. My dad _____ my lunch.

4. He _____ to me.

5. He waves to _____.

6. My _____ packs my _____.

7. He _____ to _____.

Name _____

Read the sentences under the picture. Fill in the blanks.

# Fun at School

Ted and Jane play at school.
Jane likes to swing.

1. Ted and Jane _____ at school.

2. _____ and Jane play at school.

3. Ted _____ Jane play at school.

4. _____ likes to swing.

5. Jane likes to _____.

6. Ted _____ Jane _____ at school.

7. _____ likes to _____.

Name _____

Read the sentences under the picture. Fill in the blanks.

# The Race

Ben is my brother.
I like to race him.

1. Ben is my _____.

2. _____ is my brother.

3. I like to race _____.

4. I _____ to race him.

5. I like to _____ him.

6. _____ is my _____.

7. I _____ to _____ him.

Name _____

Read the sentences under the picture. Fill in the blanks.

# Best Friends

Jake and Larry are best friends.
They love to play games.

1. Jake and Larry are _____ friends.

2. _____ and Larry are best friends.

3. Jake and Larry are _____ friends.

4. _____ love to play games.

5. They love to play _____.

6. _____ and Larry are best _____.

7. _____ love to play _____.

Name _____

Read the sentences under the picture. Fill in the blanks.

# Our Small Kitten

Our small kitten is black.
She drinks milk from a dish.

1. Our _____ kitten is black.

2. Our small kitten is _____.

3. She drinks _____ from a dish.

4. She _____ milk from a dish.

5. She drinks milk from a _____.

6. Our _____ kitten is _____.

7. She drinks _____ from a _____.

Name _____

Read and follow the directions.

Here is a dog.

Color the dog brown.

Draw a bone near the dog.

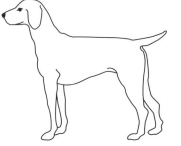

Here is a shoe.

Color the shoe yellow.

Draw another shoe near the first shoe.

Here is a car.

Color the car blue.

Draw a man next to the car.

Here is a flower.

Color the flower pink.

Draw some grass near the flower.

Name _____

Read and follow the directions.

Here is a box.

Draw a red star on the box.

Color the box yellow.

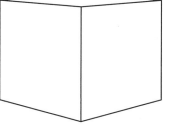

Here is a plant.

Color the plant green.

Draw three children near the plant.

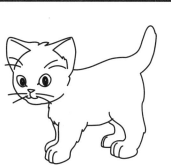

Here is a kitten.

Color the kitten black.

Draw three balls near the kitten.

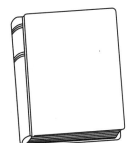

Here is a book.

Color the book red.

Draw three letters near the book.

Name _____

Read and follow the directions.

Here are three boxes.

The boxes are in Bo's room.

Color two of the boxes blue.

Put an X on the other box.

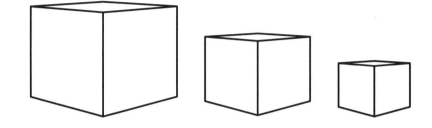

---

Here is a school.

Fran is next to the school.

Color the school red.

Put a line under Fran.

---

Here is a table.

A cat is on the table.

Color the cat green.

Put an X on the table.

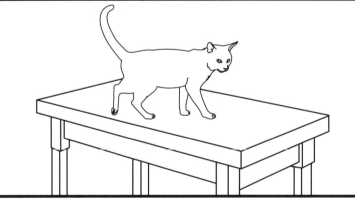

---

Here is a car.

Mom is in the car.

Color the car orange.

Circle Mom.

Name _____

Read and follow the directions.

Here is a bell.

The bell is on the table.

Put an X on the bell.

Color the table red.

___

Here are two mittens.

They are on the table.

Color the mitten on the left blue.

Circle the mitten on the right.

___

Here are three bowls.

Color the smallest bowl pink.

Put an X on the biggest bowl.

Put a line under the other bowl.

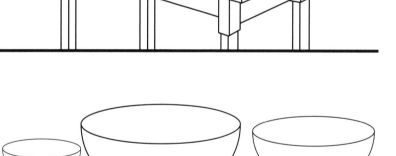

___

Here are three hats.

Color the biggest hat gold.

Circle the hat that has a star.

Put an X on the other hat.

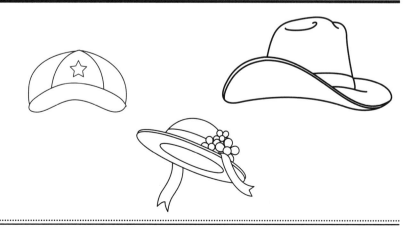

___

Name _____

Read and follow the directions.

Draw a big house.

Draw a tree near the house.

Color the tree brown and green.

Draw a fence near the house.

Draw a dog near the fence.

Draw something for the dog to play with.

Draw a boy next to the house.

Name _____

Read and follow the directions.

Draw a big tent.

Color the tent orange.

Draw two monkeys near the tent.

Color the monkeys brown or black.

Draw a white elephant in the tent.

Draw a clown in the tent.

Draw a red nose on the clown.

Name _____

Read the story. Answer the questions.

# Dan and Jill

Jill is Dan's little sister.
She likes to play with his toys.
Dan lets her use his blocks.

1. Who is Jill?

   _____

2. Who is Dan's sister?

   _____

3. Who likes to play with Dan's toys?

   _____

4. What do Jill and Dan play with?

   _____

5. Does Dan like to play with Jill?

   _____

CD-104303 • © Carson-Dellosa

Name _____

Read the story. Answer the questions.

# The Big Bug

The big bug sat on the twig.
He ate a green leaf.
The leaf was a good meal.

1. What sat on the twig?

_____

2. Where did the bug sit?

_____

3. What did the bug eat?

_____

4. What is a good meal for the bug?

_____

5. Is the bug in the story as big as a person?

_____

Name _____

Read the story. Answer the questions.

# Judy's New Doll

Judy has a new doll.
The doll's name is Mika.
Mika and Judy have blue eyes and brown hair.

1. Who is Mika?

_____

2. What does Judy have?

_____

3. Who has blue eyes?

_____

4. What color is Judy's hair?

_____

5. Does Judy look like her doll?

_____

Name _____

Read the story. Answer the questions.

# The Red Truck

Dad and Tasha have a red truck.
Dad drives her to school.
Her friend June rides with them.
They like to wave at the cars.

1. What do Dad and Tasha have?

   _____

2. What color is the truck?

   _____

3. Who does Dad drive to school?

   _____

4. Who is June?

   _____

5. What do Tasha and June like to do?

   _____

Name _____

Read the story. Answer the questions.

# Linda's Tea Party

Linda had a tea party.
Three of her friends came.
The friends were a toy bear, a doll, and a clown.
Linda gave her friends tea and oranges.

1. What did Linda have?

_____

2. Who came to the tea party?

_____

3. Who are Linda's friends?

_____

4. What did Linda give her friends?

_____

5. Did her friends really drink their tea?

_____

Name _____

Read the story. Answer the questions.

# The Dog

Jack has a new dog.
The dog is named Mel.
Mel has brown eyes and a black nose.
He wags his tail when he is happy.

1. What does Jack have?

_____

2. Who is Mel?

_____

3. What does Mel look like?

_____

4. What color is Mel's nose?

_____

5. When does Mel wag his tail?

_____

Name _____

Read the story. Answer the questions.

# The Clown

Terry's class went to a show.
A clown did funny tricks for them.
He rode a tiny bike and honked a horn.
He hit a target with a pie.
The children laughed and clapped.

1. Where did Terry's class go?

_____

2. Who did tricks in the show?

_____

3. What did the clown ride?

_____

4. Who did the clown hit with a pie?

_____

5. What did the children do?

_____

6. Did Terry's class like the show?

_____

Name _____

Read the story. Answer the questions.

# The Zoo

Ms. Soo took her class to the zoo.
The children watched monkeys play.
The monkeys made silly faces.
Then, the monkeys threw popcorn!
The class was sad to go home.

1. Who is Ms. Soo?

_____

2. Where did the class go?

_____

3. What did the children watch?

_____

4. What kind of faces did the monkeys make?

_____

5. What did the monkeys throw?

_____

6. Did the class enjoy their trip?

_____

Name _____

Read the story. Answer the questions.

# The Store

Neil likes to shop with his mother.
He pushes the cart for her.
They buy cans of fruit.
They buy cheese and meat.
Neil wants to eat lunch now.

1. Where does Neil go with his mother?

   _____

2. How does Neil feel about shopping?

   _____

3. Who pushes the cart?

   _____

4. What food is in the cans?

   _____

5. What do Neil and his mother buy?

   _____

6. What does Neil want to do now?

   _____

Name _____

Read the story. Answer the questions.

# Trip to Grandma's

Max and Lisa are going to Grandma's house.
Grandma lives in the country.
She has a lot of animals.
Max likes to feed the chickens.
Lisa wants to ride a horse.
They both love Grandma's peach pie.

1. Who are Matt and Lisa going to visit?

_____

2. Where does Grandma live?

_____

3. What does Grandma have?

_____

4. What does Max like to feed?

_____

5. What does Lisa want to ride?

_____

6. Who cooks peach pie?

_____

7. Do Max and Lisa like to eat the peach pie?

_____

Name _____

Read the story. Answer the questions.

# Sally and Beth

Sally is Beth's friend. The girls are in Mr. Garza's class. They play together after school. Sally lives down the street from Beth. They both have brothers. Sally's brother is Sam, and Beth's brother is Bob.

1. Who is Sally?

_____

2. Whose class are the two girls in?

_____

3. What do the girls do after school?

_____

4. Where does Sally live?

_____

5. What do both girls have?

_____

6. Who is Sam?

_____

7. What is the name of Beth's brother?

_____

Name _____

Read the story. Answer the questions.

# Chuck's Sad Day

Chuck was a brown squirrel. His best friend was named Lou. Lou was a black bird. Lou was flying south for the winter. All of the birds were leaving. Chuck was sad. Lou said he would see him again in the spring.

1. What was Chuck?

_____

2. Who was Lou?

_____

3. Where was Lou going?

_____

4. Who was leaving with Lou?

_____

5. How did Chuck feel?

_____

6. When will Chuck see Lou again?

_____

7. Can squirrels and birds really talk?

_____

Name _____

Read the story. Answer the questions.

# The New Car

Aunt Lil has a new car. It goes very fast. Uncle Hal drives an old truck. He takes it to the lake. He pulls his boat behind it. Aunt Lil does not want muddy shoes in her car. She would rather drive to the mall than the lake!

1. What does Aunt Lil have?

_____

2. Is Aunt Lil's car fast or slow?

_____

3. What does Uncle Hal drive?

_____

4. Where does Uncle Hal go?

_____

5. What does Uncle Hal pull?

_____

6. How does Aunt Lil feel about muddy shoes?

_____

7. Where would Aunt Lil rather go than the lake?

_____

Name _____

Read the story. Answer the questions.

# Visiting Zuru

Al likes to go to the planet Zuru. His parents came from there. Every summer they return for a visit. They pet the red lions. They eat fruit from blue trees. They swim in the orange sea. Al is sad to go home.

1. Where does Al like to go?

_____

2. When does the family visit Zuru?

_____

3. What animals does the family pet?

_____

4. What color are the fruit trees?

_____

5. Where does the family swim?

_____

6. How does Al feel when he goes home?

_____

7. Is this story real or make-believe?

_____

Name _____

Read the story. Answer the questions.

# Libby's Pet Fish

Libby went to the pet store. She wanted to get a pet. Libby looked at the mice. She looked at the hamsters and laughed. She looked at the fish. One fish looked at her and blew a bubble. Libby liked him best. She took him home with her.

1. Where did Libby go?

_____

2. What did Libby want to get?

_____

3. What animals did Libby look at?

_____

4. Which animals did Libby think were funny?

_____

5. Who blew a bubble at Libby?

_____

6. Which animal did Libby like best?

_____

7. What did Libby do with the fish?

_____

Name _____

Read the story. Answer the questions.

# Tina's Book

Tina has a book about animals. Her father reads her stories from the book. Sometimes her mother reads to her, too. Tina is learning to read. She looks at the pictures. She thinks about the animals. Soon, she will be able to read the stories herself!

1. What does Tina have?

_____

2. What does Tina's father do?

_____

3. What does Tina's mother do?

_____

4. Who is learning to read?

_____

5. What does Tina look at?

_____

6. What does Tina think about?

_____

7. When will Tina be able to read the stories herself?

_____

Name _____

Read the story. Answer the questions.

# Leo

Leo was the king of the lions. He wore a bright crown on his head. His best friend was a mouse named Moe. Moe liked to ride on Leo's back. They walked through the forest every morning. The other animals laughed when they saw a mouse with a lion.

1. Who was Leo?

   _____

2. What did Leo wear on his head?

   _____

3. Who was Leo's best friend?

   _____

4. What did Moe like to do?

   _____

5. When did Leo and Moe walk through the forest?

   _____

6. What did the other animals do when they saw Leo and Moe?

   _____

7. Is this story real or make-believe?

   _____

  CD-104303 • © Carson-Dellosa

Name _____

Read the story. Answer the questions.

# The Fair

Ozzy and Anita went to the fair. Their parents said they could ride one ride each. Ozzy rode the Ferris wheel. He pointed at his house from the top. Anita rode the bumper cars. She screamed and laughed when her car hit another one. The fair was fun for both of them!

1. Where did Ozzy and Anita go?

_____

2. How many rides could each child ride?

_____

3. What did Ozzy ride?

_____

4. What did Ozzy point at from the top?

_____

5. Who rode the bumper cars?

_____

6. Why did Anita scream and laugh?

_____

7. Did Ozzy and Anita have fun?

_____

Name _____

Read the story. Answer the questions.

# Digging Is Fun

Angie was a dog. She liked to dig holes in the ground. One day a cat named Gill came to play. Gill saw Angie digging a hole. He thought it looked like fun. Gill asked Angie if he could help. Angie said he could. She thought Gill was funny!

1. Who was Angie?

_____

2. What did Angie like to do?

_____

3. What did Gill think about digging a hole?

_____

4. What did Gill ask Angie?

_____

5. What did Angie say?

_____

6. What did Angie think about Gill?

_____

7. Is this story real or make-believe?

_____

 CD-104303 • © Carson-Dellosa

Name _____

Read the story. Answer the questions.

# The Painting

Maddie liked to paint. One day, she painted a clown with a red nose and a white face. The painting made her smile. It made her think about the circus. Maddie decided to give the painting to her teacher. It would help her remember their class trip to the circus.

1. What did Maddie like to do?

_____

2. What did Maddie paint?

_____

3. What did the clown look like?

_____

4. What did the painting make Maddie do?

_____

5. What did the painting make Maddie think about?

_____

6. Who did Maddie decide to give the painting to?

_____

7. What would the painting help Maddie's teacher remember?

_____

Name _____

Read the story. Answer the questions.

# Tigers

Tigers are very large cats. They live in places like India and China. Tigers are orange with black stripes. They like to eat meat. They have strong jaws and sharp teeth to eat their food. Today, many tigers also live in zoos. You can go see one!

1. What are two places tigers live?

   _____

2. What do tigers look like?

   _____

3. What do tigers eat?

   _____

4. Why do tigers have strong jaws and sharp teeth?

   _____

5. Where do many tigers live today?

   _____

6. Name another animal you could see at a zoo.

   _____

Name _____

Read the story. Answer the questions.

# Butterflies

Many people like butterflies because they are colorful. Some butterflies may have spots on their wings. They land on flowers and drink from them. Butterflies start out as caterpillars. Caterpillars eat leaves. Later, they grow wings and fly away!

1. Why do many people like butterflies?

_____

2. What do some butterflies have on their wings?

_____

3. Where do butterflies land?

_____

4. How do butterflies start out?

_____

5. What do caterpillars eat?

_____

6. Draw your own butterfly.

Name _____

Read the story. Answer the questions.

# Pecan Trees

Pecan trees can be found in the southern United States. The trees are tall and have green leaves. Pecans are small brown nuts. You can break open a pecan with your fingers. You can eat the nuts alone or make a pie out of them. Some people like to put pecans on their pancakes!

1. Where can you find a pecan tree?

_____

2. What do pecan trees look like?

_____

3. What do pecans look like?

_____

4. How can you break open a pecan?

_____

5. Where do some people like to put pecans?

_____

6. Name another kind of nut.

_____

Name _____

Read the story. Answer the questions.

# The Moon

The moon travels around the earth every day. We can see the moon at night. Sometimes it looks round like a ball, and sometimes it looks very thin. Some lucky people have visited the moon, but they cannot live there. People cannot breathe on the moon!

1. Where does the moon travel every day?

_____

2. When can you see the moon?

_____

3. What does the moon sometimes look like?

_____

4. Who has visited the moon?

_____

5. Why do people not live on the moon?

_____

6. Draw a picture of the moon.

Name _____

Read the story. Answer the questions.

# Skunks

Skunks are black and white. They have big, bushy tails. When a skunk is afraid, it makes a bad smell. This smell is hard to wash off. Skunks eat bugs and worms. They also like to eat plants in people's gardens. People do not like this!

1. What colors are skunks?

   _____

2. What does a skunk's tail look like?

   _____

3. What happens when a skunk is afraid?

   _____

4. What do skunks eat?

   _____

5. Why do some people not like skunks?

   _____

6. Name another animal you might see in a garden.

   _____

Name _____

Read the story. Answer the questions.

# Glass

Many things are made of glass. You can look through a glass window. You can drink from a glass cup. Be very careful! If glass breaks, it can hurt you. Some people use glass to make art. You could make a necklace with glass beads.

1. What are many things made of?

   _____

2. What can you look through?

   _____

3. What can you drink from?

   _____

4. Why should you be careful with glass?

   _____

5. What could you make with glass beads?

   _____

6. Name something else that is made from glass.

   _____

Name _____

Read the story. Answer the questions.

# Games

Some people like to play board games. They roll dice and move game pieces around the board. They may use cards to tell them what to do. The winner is the person who reaches the finish line first.

1. What do some people like to play?

_____

2. What do they roll?

_____

3. What do they move around the board?

_____

4. What might cards tell them?

_____

5. Who is the winner?

_____

6. What game do you like to play?

_____

Name _____

Read the story. Answer the questions.

# Shoes

People wear shoes to keep their feet safe. The ground could hurt your feet. You might wear special shoes for running a race. You might wear old shoes to go hiking. Some shoes have laces. Tie them tight so you do not trip!

1. Why do people wear shoes?

_____

2. What might the ground do to your feet?

_____

3. When might you wear old shoes?

_____

4. What do some shoes have?

_____

5. Why should you tie the laces tight?

_____

6. Draw a picture of your favorite shoes.

Name _____

Read the story. Answer the questions.

# The Beach

The beach has soft sand. Shells are in the sand. Fish swim in the ocean next to the beach. People like to go to the beach with their family and friends. They sit in the sun. They dip their toes into the water.

1. What does the beach have?

_____

2. Where do fish swim?

_____

3. Who do people like to go to the beach with?

_____

4. Where do they sit?

_____

5. What do people dip their toes into?

_____

6. Name another place you might go with your family.

_____

Name _____

Read the story. Answer the questions.

# Rain

Do you like to watch the rain? Rain helps plants grow. It makes flowers bloom. Your yard may be muddy after it rains. Mud is made when water mixes with dry dirt. Sometimes you can see a colorful rainbow in the sky after it rains.

1. What does the rain do?

   _____

2. What happens to flowers after it rains?

   _____

3. What might happen to your yard after it rains?

   _____

4. How is mud made?

   _____

5. What might you see in the sky after it rains?

   _____

6. Name another type of weather.

   _____

**1. Read the story.**

# Feeding the Dog

Luke has a pet dog named Kip. He feeds Kip every morning. He opens the back door and calls Kip. Kip runs to the door. Luke puts food in his bowl. Kip wags his tail and eats.

**2. Read the sentences. Rewrite them in the correct order on the lines below.**

Kip runs to the door.

Luke calls Kip.

Kip wags his tail and eats.

Luke puts food in Kip's bowl.

1. _____

2. _____

3. _____

4. _____

Name _____

## 1. Read the story.

# Cooking Soup

Clay is cooking soup. He puts a large pot on the stove. He opens a can of beans. Then, he opens a can of corn. He puts the food in the pot. Clay heats the soup. It will taste great!

## 2. Read the sentences. Rewrite them in the correct order on the lines below.

He opens the cans.
He heats the soup.
He puts the food in the pot.
He puts a pot on the stove.

1. _____

2. _____

3. _____

4. _____

Name _____

**1. Read the story.**

# Washing Clothes

Ned needs to wash his dirty clothes.
First, he sorts the colors. The white shirts go
together. He puts the clothes in the washer.
Then, he puts in the soap. When the clothes
are clean, Ned puts them in the dryer.

**2. Read the sentences. Rewrite them in the correct order on the lines below.**

He puts the clothes in the dryer.
He puts the clothes in the washer.
He sorts the colors.
He puts the soap in the washer.

1. _____

2. _____

3. _____

4. _____

CD-104303 • © Carson-Dellosa

Name _____

**I. Read the story.**

# The Big Dance

Meg's sister Susan is going to a big dance. Everyone in her class will be there. She is getting ready. She washes her hair. She puts on her dress. She pins a flower on her dress. Mom will drive her to school.

**2. Read the sentences. Rewrite them in the correct order on the lines below.**

She pins on a flower.
She washes her hair.
Mom drives her to the school.
She puts on her new dress.

I. _____

2. _____

3. _____

4. _____

Name _____

**I. Read the story.**

# Painting a Room

Dee wanted to paint her room. She and her mom went to the store to buy paint and brushes. They put on old clothes. Then, they rubbed the walls to make them smooth. They dipped the brushes in the paint. They painted the walls. Dee loves her new room!

**2. Read the sentences. Rewrite them in the correct order on the lines below.**

They put paint on the walls.
They went to the store.
They put on old clothes.
They rubbed the walls.

1. _____

2. _____

3. _____

4. _____

Name _____

**I. Read the story.**

# Emmy's Hamster

Emmy has a pet hamster. She takes good care of him. Every day she cleans his cage. Then, she feeds him grain and seeds. After that, she puts him on her lap and plays with him. She puts him back in his cage. He runs in a wheel. Emmy thinks hamsters are fun pets!

**2. Read the sentences. Rewrite them in the correct order on the lines below.**

She cleans his cage.

He runs in a wheel.

She feeds him.

She puts him back in his cage.

She plays with him.

I. _____

2. _____

3. _____

4. _____

5. _____

Name _____

**I. Read the story.**

# Mailing a Postcard

Derek wanted to send a postcard to his friend Lori. First, he found a card with a picture of a cat. Then, he wrote a note on the card. He put Lori's name and address on it. He stuck a stamp on the card and dropped it in the mailbox. Lori was happy to read the postcard!

**2. Read the sentences. Rewrite them in the correct order on the lines below.**

Derek wrote Lori's address.
Lori read the card.
Derek found a card.
Derek mailed the card.
Derek wrote a note.

1. _____

2. _____

3. _____

4. _____

5. _____

**1. Read the story.**

# Time for School

Cath is going to school for the first time. Mom tells her it is time to get up. Cath eats breakfast and brushes her teeth. She puts on a new dress. Mom helps her tie her shoes. She hands Cath a sack lunch. Then, she walks Cath to the bus stop.

**2. Read the sentences. Rewrite them in the correct order on the lines below.**

Mom walks Cath to the bus stop.
Cath puts on a dress.
Cath eats breakfast.
Mom hands Cath a sack lunch.
Mom ties Cath's shoes.

1. _____

2. _____

3. _____

4. _____

5. _____

Name _____

**I. Read the story.**

# Bedtime Story

Jon's father reads a story to him each night. Jon brushes his teeth. Then, he gets in bed, and his father sits in a chair. He reads a story and tells Jon good night. Jon dreams about the story.

**2. Read the sentences. Rewrite them in the correct order on the lines below.**

Jon's father tells him good night.
Jon brushes his teeth.
Jon dreams about the story.
Jon gets in bed.
Jon's father sits in a chair.

I. _____

2. _____

3. _____

4. _____

5. _____

Name _____

## 1. Read the story.

# Playing Tag

My friends and I played tag. We picked teams. Mimi was picked first. She is a good player. Rita ran fast in the game. It was hard to catch her. Then, Zeke hid behind a tree. We could not find him. We were tired at the end of the day. It was a fun day.

## 2. Read the sentences. Rewrite them in the correct order on the lines below.

Zeke hid behind a tree.
Rita ran fast.
We looked for Zeke.
Mimi was picked first.
We were tired.

1. _____

2. _____

3. _____

4. _____

5. _____

Name _____

**1. Read the story.**

# Fun at the Beach

Abe and Anna went to the beach. They put on their swimsuits. They put sandals on their feet. Abe ran on the soft sand. Anna chased a ball to the sea. The sun was hot, so they got in the water. They splashed each other and laughed.

**2. Read the sentences. Rewrite them in the correct order on the lines below.**

They splashed and laughed.
They put on their swimsuits.
Abe ran on the sand.
They went to the beach.
They got in the water.

1. _____

2. _____

3. _____

4. _____

5. _____

Name _____

## 1. Read the story.

# Picking a Puppy

Mom said I could get a pet. We went to the store. We looked at some puppies. A black one licked me. Then, a white one wagged its tail. It was hard to choose. We picked the little spotted puppy with the sad eyes. I will take good care of him.

**2. Read the sentences. Rewrite them in the correct order on the lines below.**

We picked the spotted puppy.
A black one licked me.
We looked at some puppies.
Mom said I could get a pet.
A white one wagged its tail.

1. _____

2. _____

3. _____

4. _____

5. _____

Name _____

## 1. Read the story.

# Our Picnic

Our family went on a picnic in the park. My brother brought a friend. Dad cooked burgers on the grill. I made a salad. Mom served ice cream after we ate. After the ice cream, we played on the swings. Mom and Dad rested under the trees. Then, we went home.

## 2. Read the sentences. Rewrite them in the correct order on the lines below.

We played on the swings.
We went home.
Dad cooked burgers.
Mom and Dad rested.
Mom served ice cream.

1. _____

2. _____

3. _____

4. _____

5. _____

Name _____

**1. Read the story.**

# Zak's Sister

Zak has a baby sister. He helps take care of her on Saturdays. In the morning, he brushes her hair. In the afternoon, he makes funny faces so she will laugh. In the evening, he feeds her. Then, he puts her to bed. Finally, Zak goes to bed. Zak's mom says Zak is a good big brother.

**2. Read the sentences. Rewrite them in the correct order on the lines below.**

Zak goes to bed.
Zak feeds her.
He makes funny faces.
He brushes her hair.
He puts her to bed.

1. _____

2. _____

3. _____

4. _____

5. _____

Name _____

**I. Read the story.**

# After School

Erin likes to go to Grandpa's after school. He picks her up at the school gate. They drive to his house. Erin hangs up her coat while Grandpa makes her a snack. She eats the food and then does her homework. Sometimes they watch TV!

**2. Read the sentences. Rewrite them in the correct order on the lines below.**

Erin does her homework.
Grandpa picks Erin up.
Erin hangs up her coat.
They drive to Grandpa's house.
Erin eats a snack.

I. _____

2. _____

3. _____

4. _____

5. _____

CD-104303 • © Carson-Dellosa

Name _____

**1. Read the story.**

# Stan's Party

Stan had a party last week. Dad baked a cake. Stan's friends came at noon. First, they played games. Then, they ate cake. After the cake, Stan opened his presents. Everyone had a great time.

**2. Read the sentences. Rewrite them in the correct order on the lines below.**

Stan opened his presents.
Dad baked a cake.
They ate cake.
They played games.
Stan's friends came.

1. _____

2. _____

3. _____

4. _____

5. _____

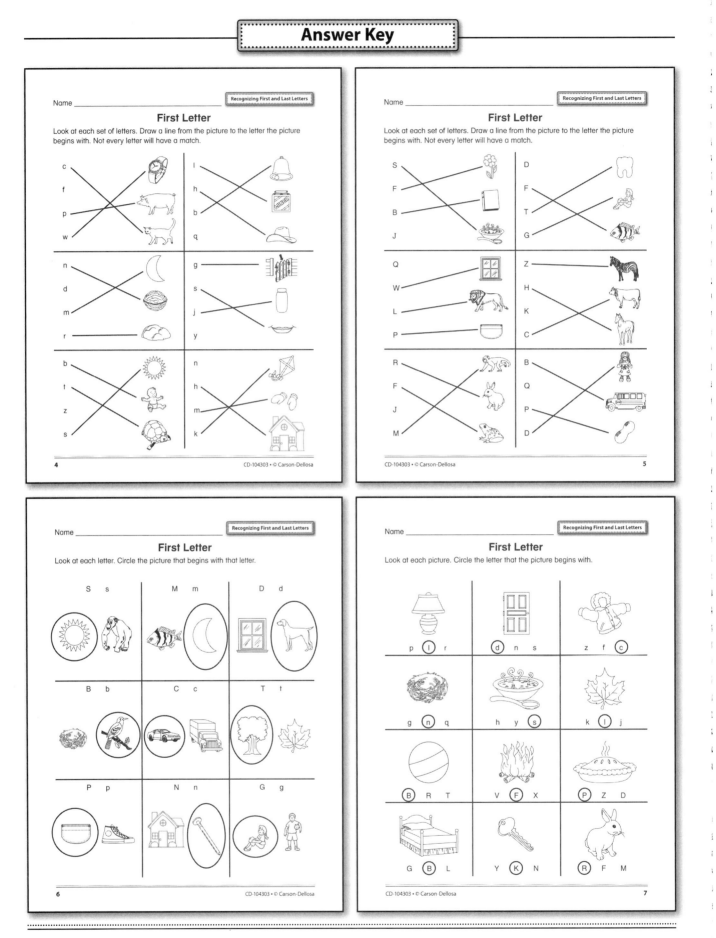

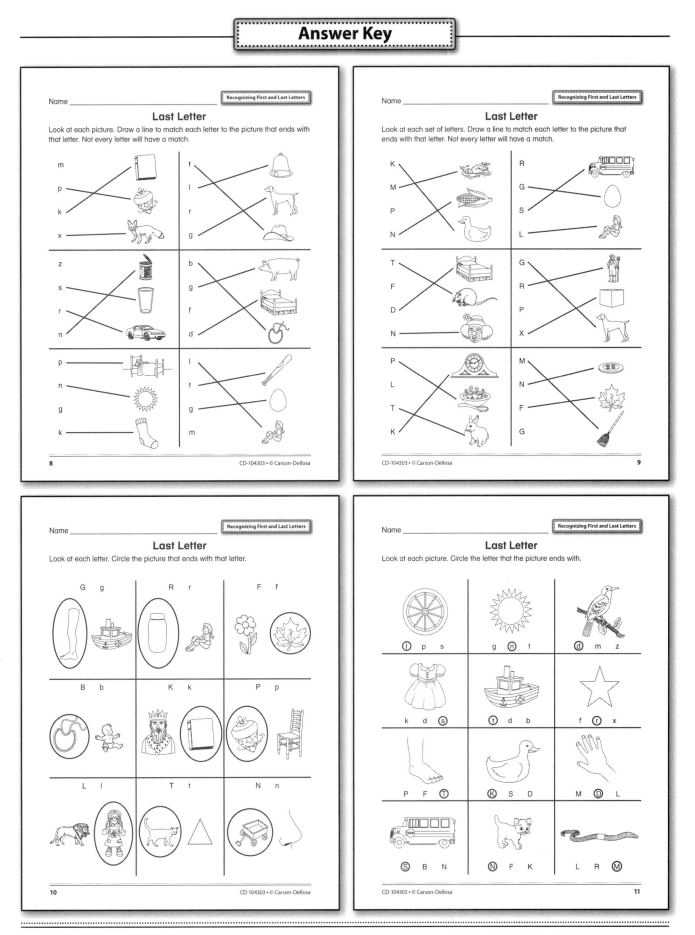

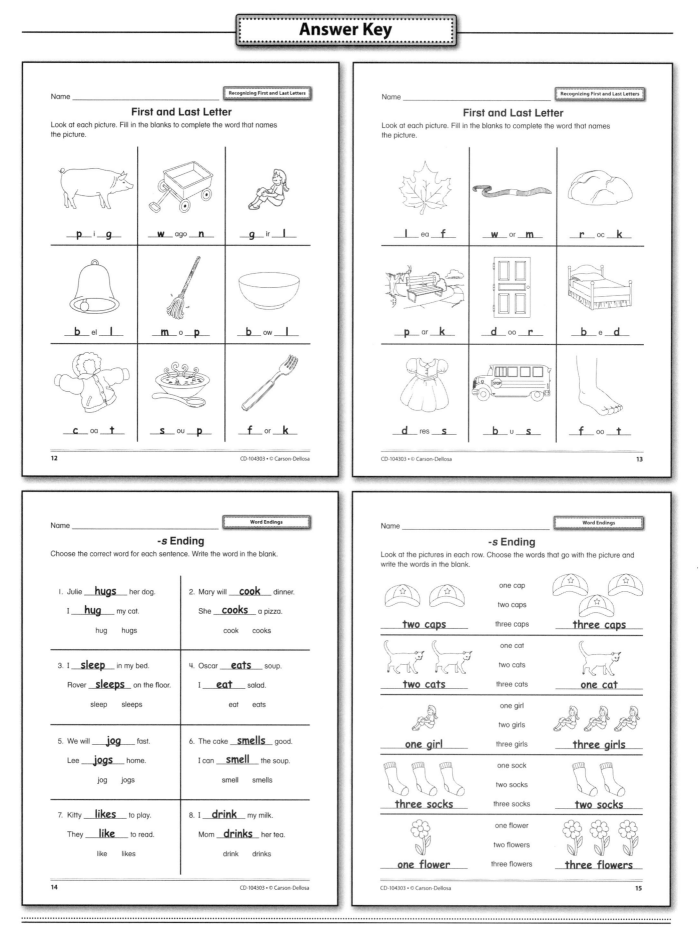

Name _____

Recognizing First and Last Letters

## First and Last Letter

Look at each picture. Fill in the blanks to complete the word that names the picture.

**p** i **g**     **w** ago **n**     **g** ir **l**

**b** el **l**     **m** o **p**     **b** ow **l**

**c** oa **t**     **s** ou **p**     **f** or **k**

12                                     CD-104303 • © Carson-Dellosa

---

Name _____

Recognizing First and Last Letters

## First and Last Letter

Look at each picture. Fill in the blanks to complete the word that names the picture.

**l** ea **f**     **w** or **m**     **r** oc **k**

**p** ar **k**     **d** oo **r**     **b** e **d**

**d** res **s**     **b** u **s**     **f** oo **t**

CD-104303 • © Carson-Dellosa                    13

---

Name _____

Word Endings

## -s Ending

Choose the correct word for each sentence. Write the word in the blank.

1. Julie **hugs** her dog.
   I **hug** my cat.
   hug     hugs

2. Mary will **cook** dinner.
   She **cooks** a pizza.
   cook     cooks

3. I **sleep** in my bed.
   Rover **sleeps** on the floor.
   sleep     sleeps

4. Oscar **eats** soup.
   I **eat** salad.
   eat     eats

5. We will **jog** fast.
   Lee **jogs** home.
   jog     jogs

6. The cake **smells** good.
   I can **smell** the soup.
   smell     smells

7. Kitty **likes** to play.
   They **like** to read.
   like     likes

8. I **drink** my milk.
   Mom **drinks** her tea.
   drink     drinks

14                                     CD-104303 • © Carson-Dellosa

---

Name _____

Word Endings

## -s Ending

Look at the pictures in each row. Choose the words that go with the picture and write the words in the blank.

one cap
two caps       **two caps**       three caps       **three caps**

one cat
two cats       **two cats**       three cats       **one cat**

one girl
two girls      **one girl**       three girls      **three girls**

one sock
two socks      **three socks**    three socks      **two socks**

one flower
two flowers    **one flower**     three flowers    **three flowers**

CD-104303 • © Carson-Dellosa                    15

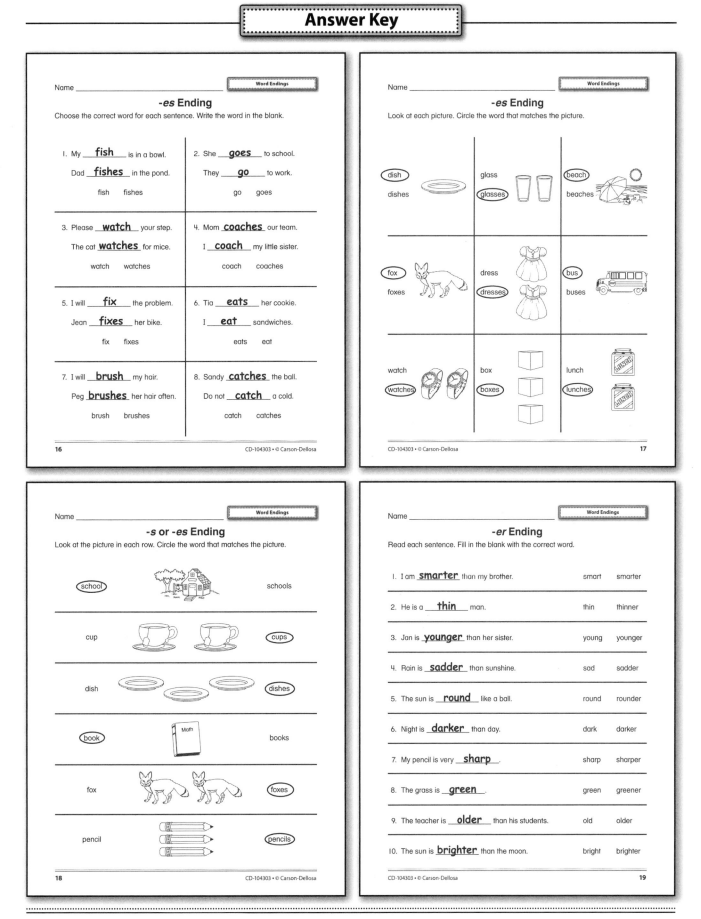

Name _____  Word Endings

## -es Ending

Choose the correct word for each sentence. Write the word in the blank.

1. My __fish__ is in a bowl.
   Dad __fishes__ in the pond.
   fish    fishes

2. She __goes__ to school.
   They __go__ to work.
   go    goes

3. Please __watch__ your step.
   The cat __watches__ for mice.
   watch    watches

4. Mom __coaches__ our team.
   I __coach__ my little sister.
   coach    coaches

5. I will __fix__ the problem.
   Jean __fixes__ her bike.
   fix    fixes

6. Tia __eats__ her cookie.
   I __eat__ sandwiches.
   eats    eat

7. I will __brush__ my hair.
   Peg __brushes__ her hair often.
   brush    brushes

8. Sandy __catches__ the ball.
   Do not __catch__ a cold.
   catch    catches

16    CD-104303 • © Carson-Dellosa

---

Name _____  Word Endings

## -es Ending

Look at each picture. Circle the word that matches the picture.

(dish) / dishes     glass / (glasses)     (beach) / beaches

(fox) / foxes     dress / (dresses)     (bus) / buses

watch / (watches)     box / (boxes)     lunch / (lunches)

CD-104303 • © Carson-Dellosa    17

---

Name _____  Word Endings

## -s or -es Ending

Look at the picture in each row. Circle the word that matches the picture.

(school)     schools

cup     (cups)

dish     (dishes)

(book)     books

fox     (foxes)

pencil     (pencils)

18    CD-104303 • © Carson-Dellosa

---

Name _____  Word Endings

## -er Ending

Read each sentence. Fill in the blank with the correct word.

1. I am __smarter__ than my brother.        smart    smarter

2. He is a __thin__ man.        thin    thinner

3. Jan is __younger__ than her sister.        young    younger

4. Rain is __sadder__ than sunshine.        sad    sadder

5. The sun is __round__ like a ball.        round    rounder

6. Night is __darker__ than day.        dark    darker

7. My pencil is very __sharp__.        sharp    sharper

8. The grass is __green__.        green    greener

9. The teacher is __older__ than his students.        old    older

10. The sun is __brighter__ than the moon.        bright    brighter

CD-104303 • © Carson-Dellosa    19

Name _____

Word Endings

### -ed Ending
Read each sentence. Fill in the blank with the correct word.

1. The rabbit **hopped** in the grass. | hop | hopped
2. I will **clean** my room. | clean | cleaned
3. Mom **looked** for a new car. | look | looked
4. We **laughed** when he told a joke. | laugh | laughed
5. Nan **spilled** her milk. | spill | spilled
6. Please **circle** the right answer. | circle | circled
7. Dad **fished** at the lake. | fish | fished
8. Mike **walked** to school this morning. | walk | walked
9. I **rolled** the ball to her a minute ago. | roll | rolled
10. Kate **fixed** her car last week. | fix | fixed

20     CD-104303 • © Carson-Dellosa

---

Name _____

Word Endings

### -er or -ed Ending
Read each sentence. Fill in the blank with the correct word.

1. The barn is **redder** than the house. | red | redder
2. Grandma **stepped** carefully onto the ladder. | step | stepped
3. The tree was as **tall** as the child. | tall | taller
4. This box is **lighter** than that one. | light | lighter
5. She **patted** the dog on the head. | pat | patted
6. I like to **walk** to the store. | walk | walked
7. The **long** snake moves in the grass. | long | longer
8. Matt **jumped** off the high board. | jump | jumped
9. We want to **row** down the river. | row | rowed
10. The kitten is **smaller** than the cat. | small | smaller

CD-104303 • © Carson-Dellosa     21

---

Name _____

Word Endings

### -er or -ed Ending
Read each sentence. Fill in the blank with the correct word.

1. Please **finish** your work. | finish | finished
2. Ms. Dove is my **teacher**. | teach | teacher
3. The **boxer** stepped into the ring. | box | boxer
4. Pete is a good **cook**. | cook | cooked
5. We will **learn** to play soccer. | learn | learned
6. Mary **skipped** down the sidewalk. | skip | skipped
7. I am a good **reader**. | read | reader
8. We **own** a farm. | own | owner
9. Please **move** to the next chair. | move | moved
10. My pony is very **fast**. | fast | faster

22     CD-104303 • © Carson-Dellosa

---

Name _____

Classifying

### Synonyms
For each sentence, read the list of words. Circle the word that means almost the same thing as the underlined word.

1. I was glad to finish the test. | (happy) | mad | warm
2. Sue and Rick like to talk. | run | (speak) | swim
3. You did a nice job. | bad | (great) | wide
4. Fred's boots got wet in the rain. | hands | books | (shoes)
5. Alice has three children. | (kids) | animals | friends
6. Tom is afraid of dogs. | angry | (scared) | cats
7. We used glue in art class. | paper | paint | (paste)
8. Aunt Ellen has a beautiful house. | (pretty) | home | big

CD-104303 • © Carson-Dellosa     23

## Synonyms

Name _____

Classifying

For each sentence, read the list of words. Circle the word that means almost the same thing as the underlined word.

| | | | |
|---|---|---|---|
| 1. Please shut the door. | open | (close) | window |
| 2. You can fold the paper in half. | (bend) | flower | pen |
| 3. Jo's bag is full of books. | bat | (sack) | table |
| 4. Dad will bake a cake. | (cook) | eat | cut |
| 5. I want a small lunch. | dinner | big | (little) |
| 6. A rabbit is quick. | (fast) | brown | quiet |
| 7. Dave will begin the song. | (start) | end | sing |
| 8. My dad won first place. | (father) | mom | game |

24     CD-104303 • © Carson-Dellosa

## Antonyms

Name _____

Classifying

Read each list of words. Circle the word that is the opposite of the first word.

| | | | |
|---|---|---|---|
| 1. **night** | sleep | (day) | sun |
| 2. **thick** | (thin) | white | wide |
| 3. **quick** | fast | quiet | (slow) |
| 4. **always** | (never) | time | short |
| 5. **sad** | (happy) | smile | blue |
| 6. **high** | tall | tree | (low) |
| 7. **hot** | warm | (cold) | ice |
| 8. **leave** | (return) | go | sleep |

CD-104303 • © Carson-Dellosa     25

## Antonyms

Name _____

Classifying

Read each list of words. Circle the word that is the opposite of the first word.

| | | | |
|---|---|---|---|
| 1. **quiet** | (loud) | soft | hard |
| 2. **good** | (bad) | nice | sad |
| 3. **new** | hot | (old) | quiet |
| 4. **yes** | not | (no) | maybe |
| 5. **right** | (wrong) | good | write |
| 6. **scream** | talk | cry | (whisper) |
| 7. **alike** | (different) | love | pair |
| 8. **sunny** | hot | (rainy) | summer |

26     CD-104303 • © Carson-Dellosa

## What Is It?

Name _____

Classifying

Read each question. Circle the word that answers the question. Use the word in a sentence that answers the question.

1. What is small?    house    school    (kitten)

   A kitten is small.

2. What is hard?    sock    milk    (rock)

   A rock is hard.

3. What smells good?    socks    book    (flower)

   A flower smells good.

4. What can you open?    rug    (window)    king

   You can open a window.

5. What shines at night?    (moon)    sun    bed

   The moon shines at night.

6. What lives in water?    (fish)    basketball    clown

   A fish lives in water.

CD-104303 • © Carson-Dellosa     27

## What Is It?

Name _____  Classifying

Read each question. Circle the word that answers the question. Use the word in a sentence that answers the question.

1. What can a horse do?   cook   (race)   whisper

**A horse can race.**

2. What can you cook?   (soup)   kitchen   shovel

**You can cook soup.**

3. What do you sleep on?   table   basket   (bed)

**You sleep on a bed.**

4. What has stripes?   (zebra)   lion   crown

**A zebra has stripes.**

5. What tastes sweet?   (cake)   dish   meat

**Cake tastes sweet.**

6. What can you wear?   picnic   cat   (clothes)

**You can wear clothes.**

28    CD-104303 • © Carson-Dellosa

## What Am I?

Name _____  Classifying

Read the clues for each riddle. Circle the correct answer.

| I am long. I have a point. I help you write. What am I? | I can fly. I have pretty wings. I sip from flowers. What am I? |
|---|---|
| book   (pencil) | chicken   grass |
| math   teacher | (butterfly)   horse |
| I am orange. I am round. I have a green stem. What am I? | I climb trees. I make funny faces. I hang by my tail. What am I? |
| (pumpkin)   spoon | (monkey)   goat |
| house   apple | dog   bird |
| I have two wheels. I can go fast. Children can ride me. What am I? | I am round. I am full of air. I float in the sky. What am I? |
| car   (bike) | coat   bone |
| horse   truck | ball   (balloon) |

CD-104303 • © Carson-Dellosa    29

## What Am I?

Name _____  Classifying

Read the clues for each riddle. Circle the correct answer.

| I am brown or gray. I have a big tail. I eat acorns. What am I? | I am round. I can be many colors. I help you see. What am I? |
|---|---|
| tree   shell | ears   (eyes) |
| (squirrel)   cat | nose   face |
| I have four legs. I am made of wood or metal. I belong at a table. What am I? | I am large. I can swim. I live in the sea. What am I? |
| (chair)   teacher | boat   goldfish |
| tree   bird | water   (whale) |
| I am soft. I have sheets. I help you rest. What am I? | I am fluffy. I live in the sky. I can be white, gray, or black. What am I? |
| (bed)   jeans | sun   moon |
| floor   home | (cloud)   drop |

30    CD-104303 • © Carson-Dellosa

## What Does Not Belong?

Name _____  Classifying

Read each list of words. Circle the word that does not go with the others.

1. apple   orange   banana   (glass)

2. mother   father   (elephant)   son

3. five   (clock)   six   two

4. whale   shark   dolphin   (swim)

5. flower   (bow)   plant   seed

6. fork   spoon   knife   (grass)

7. hair   eyes   (turtle)   nose

8. read   (finger)   study   play

CD-104303 • © Carson-Dellosa    31

## What Does Not Belong?

Name _____

Classifying

Read each list of words. Circle the word that does not go with the others.

1. pencil    crayon    (paper)    pen

2. mug    cup    glass    (table)

3. class    (farm)    school    teacher

4. sun    star    (grass)    moon

5. yellow    (car)    orange    blue

6. sit    stand    (chair)    lie

7. king    prince    queen    (frog)

8. coat    (rose)    pants    shirt

32    CD-104303 • © Carson-Dellosa

---

## Yes or No?

Name _____

Classifying

Read each sentence. Decide whether it is true. Circle yes or no.

Yes         (No)

A kitten can fly.

| A school can jump. | Yes | (No) |
| Pigs can eat. | (Yes) | No |
| All horses are white. | Yes | (No) |
| Kids can walk down the street. | (Yes) | No |

| All books are short. | Yes | (No) |
| A fox can speak. | Yes | (No) |
| You can roll a ball. | (Yes) | No |
| Boys can sing songs. | (Yes) | No |

| A snail can run. | Yes | (No) |
| All rabbits are big. | Yes | (No) |
| A plane is faster than a car. | (Yes) | No |
| The moon is green. | Yes | (No) |

CD-104303 • © Carson-Dellosa    33

---

## Yes or No?

Name _____

Classifying

Read each sentence. Decide whether it is true. Circle yes or no.

(Yes)         No

A girl can go to school.

| The sun gives us light. | (Yes) | No |
| All puppies are huge. | Yes | (No) |
| Cars can go to work. | (Yes) | No |
| Children can do math. | (Yes) | No |

| Teams always win. | Yes | (No) |
| Pencils can be sharp. | (Yes) | No |
| Fish can read. | Yes | (No) |
| All houses are blue. | Yes | (No) |

| A door can be made of wood. | (Yes) | No |
| All crayons are red. | Yes | (No) |
| A frog can hop. | (Yes) | No |
| A snake can walk. | Yes | (No) |

34    CD-104303 • © Carson-Dellosa

---

## Rhymes

Name _____

Classifying

Read each list of words. Circle the words that rhyme with the first word.

1. **jig**    jug    (fig)    (pig)    jog    (big)

2. **sap**    sip    (map)    (tap)    stop    (trap)

3. **vine**    (fine)    tree    (line)    (pine)    vet

4. **ball**    bell    (wall)    (tall)    bowl    (hall)

5. **hot**    (tot)    cold    warm    (cot)    (not)

6. **pail**    pill    (nail)    (sail)    pile    (tail)

7. **old**    young    (fold)    (cold)    age    (sold)

8. **pat**    (sat)    (that)    get    pet    (cat)

CD-104303 • © Carson-Dellosa    35

---

Name _____ | Classifying

### Rhymes

Read each list of words. Circle the words that rhyme with the first word.

1. **glass** — (pass) gloss milk (mass) (class)

2. **most** — (post) (toast) tall bed (host)

3. **neat** — messy (meat) clean (beat) (heat)

4. **tan** — (can) white (ran) (plan) sun

5. **stool** — chair (cool) (pool) sit (fool)

6. **pen** — (hen) (den) pencil paper (ten)

7. **gate** — (late) (slate) door (skate) lock

8. **bad** — (dad) (sad) beam grade (lad)

36    CD-104303 • © Carson-Dellosa

---

Name _____ | Classifying

### Multiple Meanings

Look at the pictures. Draw a line to match each picture with the correct sentence.

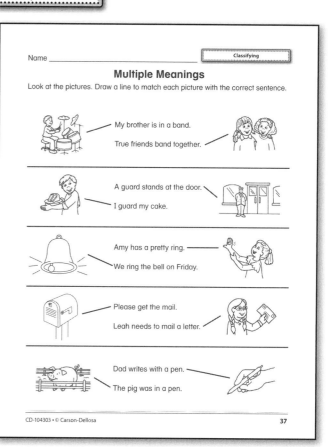

My brother is in a band.
True friends band together.

A guard stands at the door.
I guard my cake.

Amy has a pretty ring.
We ring the bell on Friday.

Please get the mail.
Leah needs to mail a letter.

Dad writes with a pen.
The pig was in a pen.

CD-104303 • © Carson-Dellosa    37

---

Name _____ | Context

### Find the Right Word

Read each sentence. Fill in the blank with the correct word to complete the sentence.

1. Jerry __gave__ me a new pencil. | give | gave

2. We __sailed__ our toy boat. | sailed | sails

3. Mom and Dad __went__ to the store. | goes | went

4. Penny __met__ an old friend. | meet | met

5. Ali __saw__ the eagle fly above her. | saw | seen

6. Gina __became__ a good student. | become | became

7. I __have__ a baby sister. | has | have

8. We __thank__ you for coming. | thank | thanks

9. A plane __flies__ high. | fly | flies

10. The sun __was__ shining. | were | was

38    CD-104303 • © Carson-Dellosa

---

Name _____ | Context

### Find the Right Word

Read each sentence. Fill in the blank with the correct word to complete the sentence.

1. Ray __listens__ well. | listen | listens

2. She __loves__ to play tag. | loves | love

3. Sheri can __swim__ ten laps. | swam | swim

4. Jen __watched__ the circus show. | watch | watched

5. He __dried__ the wet shirt. | dried | dry

6. My brother __played__ in the park. | played | play

7. I __took__ the last cookie. | takes | took

8. Phil __was__ late. | am | was

9. Monkeys __make__ me laugh. | make | makes

10. Trina __has__ a blue ring. | have | has

CD-104303 • © Carson-Dellosa    39

---

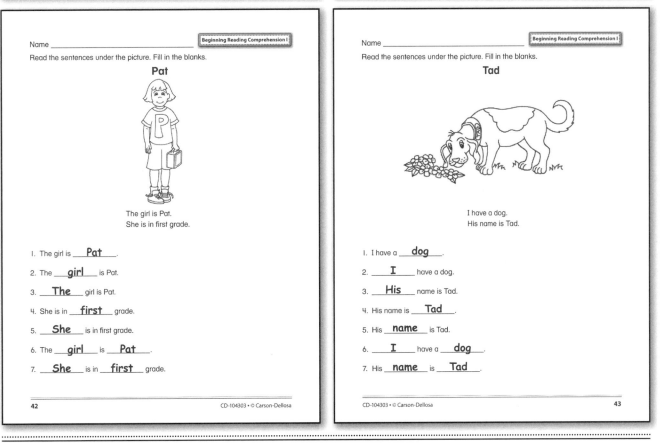

Name _____    Context

## Find the Right Word

Read each sentence. Fill in the blank with the correct word to complete the sentence.

1. Mom __wore__ her gold necklace.    wear    wore

2. Pam __is__ my best friend.    are    is

3. We __like__ to draw.    like    likes

4. The dog __ran__ to her.    run    ran

5. Mr. Ang __told__ a story.    told    tell

6. I __hugged__ Dad good-bye.    hugs    hugged

7. That puppy __eats__ a lot.    eat    eats

8. The road __was__ bumpy.    was    were

9. Her car __goes__ too slowly.    goes    go

10. Mark __wants__ his lunch.    want    wants

40    CD-104303 • © Carson-Dellosa

---

Name _____    Context

## Find the Right Word

Read each sentence. Fill in the blank with the correct word to complete the sentence.

1. My friend read ten __books__.    books    book

2. Her __mother__ played with her.    mothers    mother

3. Ten __clowns__ rode in the car.    clown    clowns

4. One __team__ will win.    teams    team

5. Paul likes to tell __jokes__.    joke    jokes

6. I have two __dimes__ in my pocket.    dime    dimes

7. Harry has six __parrots__.    parrots    parrot

8. Their family has two __vans__.    van    vans

9. Our town has one __pool__.    pool    pools

10. Todd ate three __pieces__ of pie.    pieces    piece

CD-104303 • © Carson-Dellosa    41

---

Name _____    Beginning Reading Comprehension I

Read the sentences under the picture. Fill in the blanks.

### Pat

The girl is Pat.
She is in first grade.

1. The girl is __Pat__.

2. The __girl__ is Pat.

3. __The__ girl is Pat.

4. She is in __first__ grade.

5. __She__ is in first grade.

6. The __girl__ is __Pat__.

7. __She__ is in __first__ grade.

42    CD-104303 • © Carson-Dellosa

---

Name _____    Beginning Reading Comprehension I

Read the sentences under the picture. Fill in the blanks.

### Tad

I have a dog.
His name is Tad.

1. I have a __dog__.

2. __I__ have a dog.

3. __His__ name is Tad.

4. His name is __Tad__.

5. His __name__ is Tad.

6. __I__ have a __dog__.

7. His __name__ is __Tad__.

CD-104303 • © Carson-Dellosa    43

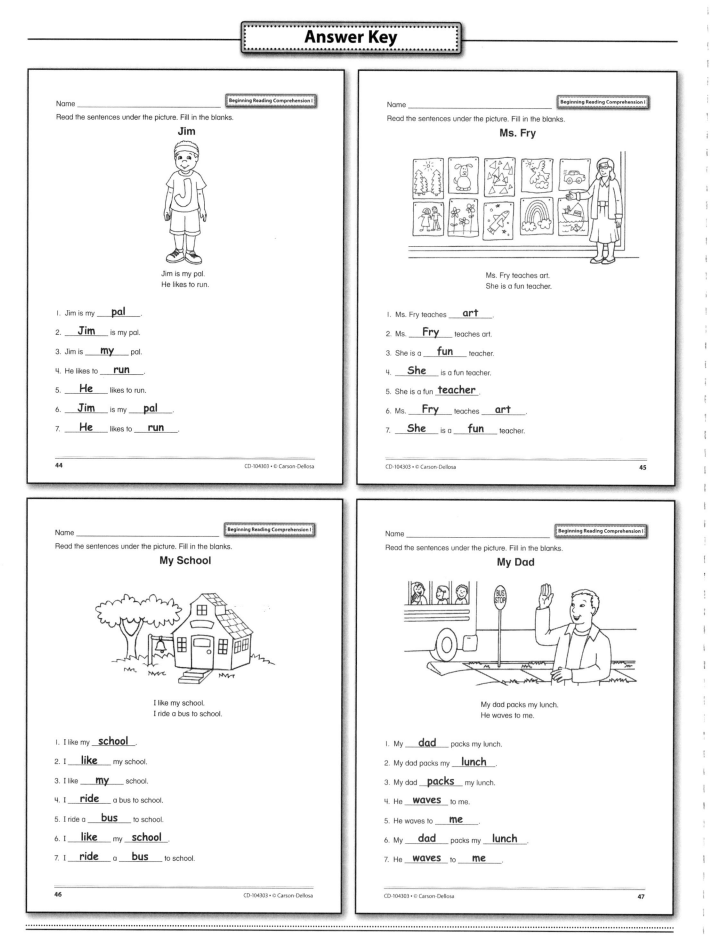

Name _____

Beginning Reading Comprehension I

Read the sentences under the picture. Fill in the blanks.

**Jim**

Jim is my pal.
He likes to run.

1. Jim is my ___**pal**___.
2. ___**Jim**___ is my pal.
3. Jim is ___**my**___ pal.
4. He likes to ___**run**___.
5. ___**He**___ likes to run.
6. ___**Jim**___ is my ___**pal**___.
7. ___**He**___ likes to ___**run**___.

44                          CD-104303 • © Carson-Dellosa

---

Name _____

Beginning Reading Comprehension I

Read the sentences under the picture. Fill in the blanks.

**Ms. Fry**

Ms. Fry teaches art.
She is a fun teacher.

1. Ms. Fry teaches ___**art**___.
2. Ms. ___**Fry**___ teaches art.
3. She is a ___**fun**___ teacher.
4. ___**She**___ is a fun teacher.
5. She is a fun ___**teacher**___.
6. Ms. ___**Fry**___ teaches ___**art**___.
7. ___**She**___ is a ___**fun**___ teacher.

CD-104303 • © Carson-Dellosa                          45

---

Name _____

Beginning Reading Comprehension I

Read the sentences under the picture. Fill in the blanks.

**My School**

I like my school.
I ride a bus to school.

1. I like my ___**school**___.
2. I ___**like**___ my school.
3. I like ___**my**___ school.
4. I ___**ride**___ a bus to school.
5. I ride a ___**bus**___ to school.
6. I ___**like**___ my ___**school**___.
7. I ___**ride**___ a ___**bus**___ to school.

46                          CD-104303 • © Carson-Dellosa

---

Name _____

Beginning Reading Comprehension I

Read the sentences under the picture. Fill in the blanks.

**My Dad**

My dad packs my lunch.
He waves to me.

1. My ___**dad**___ packs my lunch.
2. My dad packs my ___**lunch**___.
3. My dad ___**packs**___ my lunch.
4. He ___**waves**___ to me.
5. He waves to ___**me**___.
6. My ___**dad**___ packs my ___**lunch**___.
7. He ___**waves**___ to ___**me**___.

CD-104303 • © Carson-Dellosa                          47

---

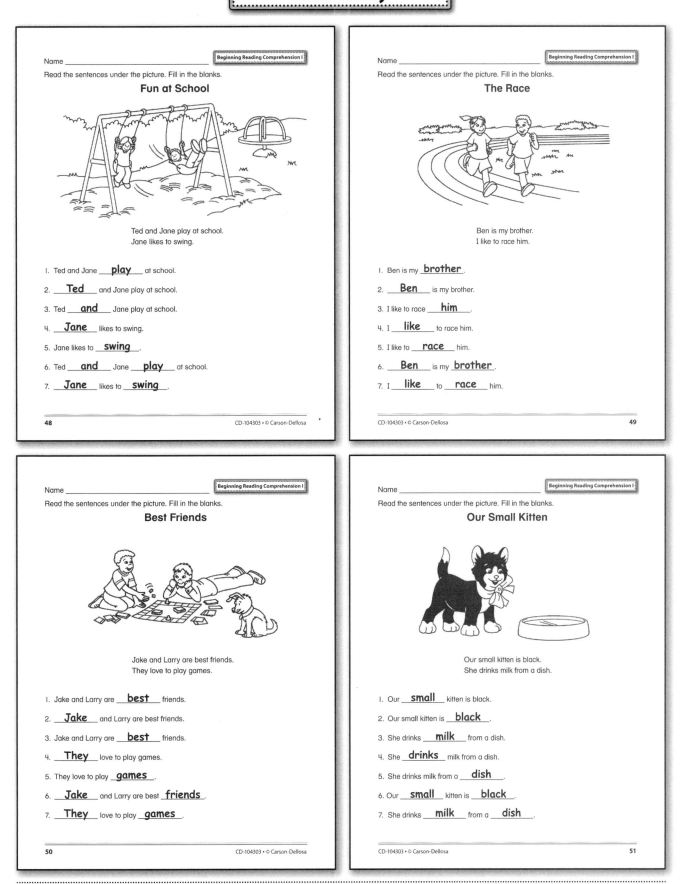

Name _____

Beginning Reading Comprehension I

Read the sentences under the picture. Fill in the blanks.

## Fun at School

Ted and Jane play at school.
Jane likes to swing.

1. Ted and Jane __play__ at school.

2. __Ted__ and Jane play at school.

3. Ted __and__ Jane play at school.

4. __Jane__ likes to swing.

5. Jane likes to __swing__.

6. Ted __and__ Jane __play__ at school.

7. __Jane__ likes to __swing__.

48                     CD-104303 • © Carson-Dellosa

---

Name _____

Beginning Reading Comprehension I

Read the sentences under the picture. Fill in the blanks.

## The Race

Ben is my brother.
I like to race him.

1. Ben is my __brother__.

2. __Ben__ is my brother.

3. I like to race __him__.

4. I __like__ to race him.

5. I like to __race__ him.

6. __Ben__ is my __brother__.

7. I __like__ to __race__ him.

CD-104303 • © Carson-Dellosa                     49

---

Name _____

Beginning Reading Comprehension I

Read the sentences under the picture. Fill in the blanks.

## Best Friends

Jake and Larry are best friends.
They love to play games.

1. Jake and Larry are __best__ friends.

2. __Jake__ and Larry are best friends.

3. Jake and Larry are __best__ friends.

4. __They__ love to play games.

5. They love to play __games__.

6. __Jake__ and Larry are best __friends__.

7. __They__ love to play __games__.

50                     CD-104303 • © Carson-Dellosa

---

Name _____

Beginning Reading Comprehension I

Read the sentences under the picture. Fill in the blanks.

## Our Small Kitten

Our small kitten is black.
She drinks milk from a dish.

1. Our __small__ kitten is black.

2. Our small kitten is __black__.

3. She drinks __milk__ from a dish.

4. She __drinks__ milk from a dish.

5. She drinks milk from a __dish__.

6. Our __small__ kitten is __black__.

7. She drinks __milk__ from a __dish__.

CD-104303 • © Carson-Dellosa                     51

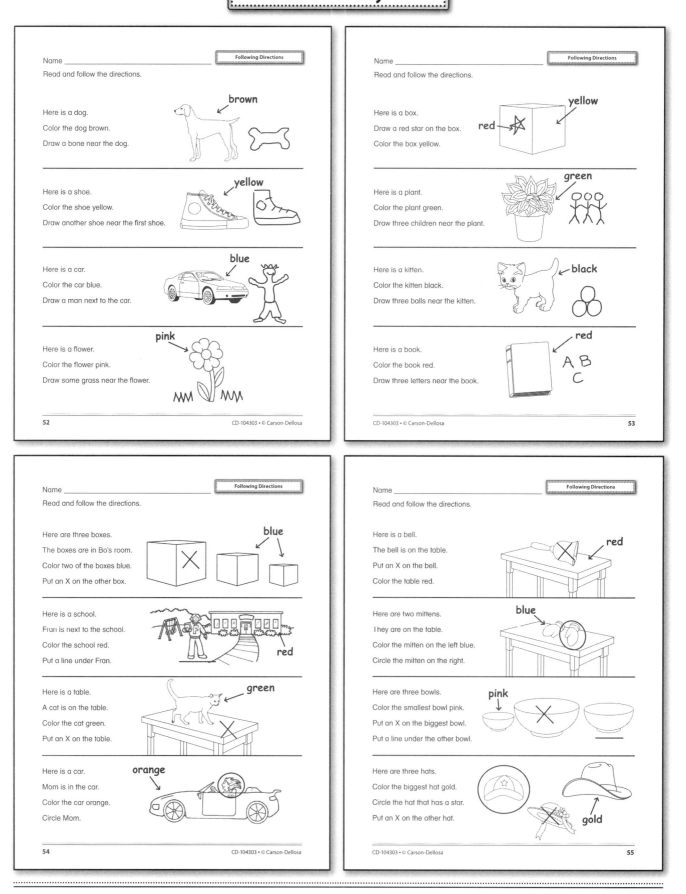

Name _____

Read and follow the directions.

Draw a big house.
Draw a tree near the house.
Color the tree brown and green.
Draw a fence near the house.
Draw a dog near the fence.
Draw something for the dog to play with.
Draw a boy next to the house.

56    CD-104303 • © Carson-Dellosa

Name _____

Read and follow the directions.

Draw a big tent.
Color the tent orange.
Draw two monkeys near the tent.
Color the monkeys brown or black.
Draw a white elephant in the tent.
Draw a clown in the tent.
Draw a red nose on the clown.

CD-104303 • © Carson-Dellosa    57

Name _____

Read the story. Answer the questions.

### Dan and Jill

Jill is Dan's little sister.
She likes to play with his toys.
Dan lets her use his blocks.

1. Who is Jill?
   **Dan's sister**

2. Who is Dan's sister?
   **Jill**

3. Who likes to play with Dan's toys?
   **Jill and Dan**

4. What do Jill and Dan play with?
   **blocks or toys**

5. Does Dan like to play with Jill?
   **yes**

58    CD-104303 • © Carson-Dellosa

Name _____

Read the story. Answer the questions.

### The Big Bug

The big bug sat on the twig.
He ate a green leaf.
The leaf was a good meal.

1. What sat on the twig?
   **the big bug**

2. Where did the bug sit?
   **on the twig**

3. What did the bug eat?
   **a green leaf**

4. What is a good meal for the bug?
   **the leaf**

5. Is the bug in the story as big as a person?
   **no**

CD-104303 • © Carson-Dellosa    59

---

Name _____

Beginning Reading Comprehension II

Read the story. Answer the questions.

### Judy's New Doll

Judy has a new doll.
The doll's name is Mika.
Mika and Judy have blue eyes and brown hair.

1. Who is Mika?
   **Judy's new doll**

2. What does Judy have?
   **a new doll**

3. Who has blue eyes?
   **Mika and Judy**

4. What color is Judy's hair?
   **brown**

5. Does Judy look like her doll?
   **yes**

60                          CD-104303 • © Carson-Dellosa

---

Name _____

Beginning Reading Comprehension II

Read the story. Answer the questions.

### The Red Truck

Dad and Tasha have a red truck.
Dad drives her to school.
Her friend June rides with them.
They like to wave at the cars.

1. What do Dad and Tasha have?
   **a red truck**

2. What color is the truck?
   **red**

3. Who does Dad drive to school?
   **Tasha and June**

4. Who is June?
   **Tasha's friend**

5. What do Tasha and June like to do?
   **wave at cars**

CD-104303 • © Carson-Dellosa                          61

---

Name _____

Beginning Reading Comprehension II

Read the story. Answer the questions.

### Linda's Tea Party

Linda had a tea party.
Three of her friends came.
The friends were a toy bear, a doll, and a clown.
Linda gave her friends tea and oranges.

1. What did Linda have?
   **a tea party**

2. Who came to the tea party?
   **three of Linda's friends**

3. Who are Linda's friends?
   **a toy bear, a doll, and a clown**

4. What did Linda give her friends?
   **tea and oranges**

5. Did her friends really drink their tea?
   **no**

62                          CD-104303 • © Carson-Dellosa

---

Name _____

Beginning Reading Comprehension II

Read the story. Answer the questions.

### The Dog

Jack has a new dog.
The dog is named Mel.
Mel has brown eyes and a black nose.
He wags his tail when he is happy.

1. What does Jack have?
   **a new dog**

2. Who is Mel?
   **Jack's new dog**

3. What does Mel look like?
   **has brown eyes**

4. What color is Mel's nose?
   **black**

5. When does Mel wag his tail?
   **when he is happy**

CD-104303 • © Carson-Dellosa                          63

---

## The Clown

Name _____

Beginning Reading Comprehension II

Read the story. Answer the questions.

Terry's class went to a show.
A clown did funny tricks for them.
He rode a tiny bike and honked a horn.
He hit a target with a pie.
The children laughed and clapped.

1. Where did Terry's class go?
   **a show**
2. Who did tricks in the show?
   **a clown**
3. What did the clown ride?
   **a tiny bike**
4. Who did the clown hit with a pie?
   **a target**
5. What did the children do?
   **laugh and clap**
6. Did Terry's class like the show?
   **yes**

64  CD-104303 • © Carson-Dellosa

## The Zoo

Name _____

Beginning Reading Comprehension II

Read the story. Answer the questions.

Ms. Soo took her class to the zoo.
The children watched monkeys play.
The monkeys made silly faces.
Then, the monkeys threw popcorn!
The class was sad to go home.

1. Who is Ms. Soo?
   **a teacher**
2. Where did the class go?
   **the zoo**
3. What did the children watch?
   **the monkeys**
4. What kind of faces did the monkeys make?
   **silly**
5. What did the monkeys throw?
   **popcorn**
6. Did the class enjoy their trip?
   **yes**

CD-104303 • © Carson-Dellosa  65

## The Store

Name _____

Beginning Reading Comprehension II

Read the story. Answer the questions.

Neil likes to shop with his mother.
He pushes the cart for her.
They buy cans of fruit.
They buy cheese and meat.
Neil wants to eat lunch now.

1. Where does Neil go with his mother?
   **the store**
2. How does Neil feel about shopping?
   **He likes it.**
3. Who pushes the cart?
   **Neil**
4. What food is in the cans?
   **fruit**
5. What do Neil and his mother buy?
   **cans of fruit, cheese, and meat**
6. What does Neil want to do now?
   **eat lunch**

66  CD-104303 • © Carson-Dellosa

## Trip to Grandma's

Name _____

Beginning Reading Comprehension II

Read the story. Answer the questions.

Max and Lisa are going to Grandma's house.
Grandma lives in the country.
She has a lot of animals.
Max likes to feed the chickens.
Lisa wants to ride a horse.
They both love Grandma's peach pie.

1. Who are Matt and Lisa going to visit?
   **Grandma**
2. Where does Grandma live?
   **in the country**
3. What does Grandma have?
   **a lot of animals**
4. What does Max like to feed?
   **the chickens**
5. What does Lisa want to ride?
   **a horse**
6. Who cooks peach pie?
   **Grandma**
7. Do Max and Lisa like to eat the peach pie?
   **yes**

CD-104303 • © Carson-Dellosa  67

Name _____

Read the story. Answer the questions.

### Sally and Beth

Sally is Beth's friend. The girls are in Mr. Garza's class. They play together after school. Sally lives down the street from Beth. They both have brothers. Sally's brother is Sam, and Beth's brother is Bob.

1. Who is Sally?
   **Beth's friend**

2. Whose class are the two girls in?
   **Mr. Garza's**

3. What do the girls do after school?
   **play together**

4. Where does Sally live?
   **down the street from Beth**

5. What do both girls have?
   **brothers**

6. Who is Sam?
   **Sally's brother**

7. What is the name of Beth's brother?
   **Bob**

68       CD-104303 • © Carson-Dellosa

---

Name _____

Read the story. Answer the questions.

### Chuck's Sad Day

Chuck was a brown squirrel. His best friend was named Lou. Lou was a black bird. Lou was flying south for the winter. All of the birds were leaving. Chuck was sad. Lou said he would see him again in the spring.

1. What was Chuck?
   **a brown squirrel**

2. Who was Lou?
   **Chuck's best friend; a bird**

3. Where was Lou going?
   **south for the winter**

4. Who was leaving with Lou?
   **all of the birds**

5. How did Chuck feel?
   **sad**

6. When will Chuck see Lou again?
   **in the spring**

7. Can squirrels and birds really talk?
   **no**

CD-104303 • © Carson-Dellosa       69

---

Name _____

Read the story. Answer the questions.

### The New Car

Aunt Lil has a new car. It goes very fast. Uncle Hal drives an old truck. He takes it to the lake. He pulls his boat behind it. Aunt Lil does not want muddy shoes in her car. She would rather drive to the mall than the lake!

1. What does Aunt Lil have?
   **a new car**

2. Is Aunt Lil's car fast or slow?
   **fast**

3. What does Uncle Hal drive?
   **an old truck**

4. Where does Uncle Hal go?
   **the lake**

5. What does Uncle Hal pull?
   **his boat**

6. How does Aunt Lil feel about muddy shoes?
   **She does not want them in her car.**

7. Where would Aunt Lil rather go than the lake?
   **to the mall**

70       CD-104303 • © Carson-Dellosa

---

Name _____

Read the story. Answer the questions.

### Visiting Zuru

Al likes to go to the planet Zuru. His parents came from there. Every summer they return for a visit. They pet the red lions. They eat fruit from blue trees. They swim in the orange sea. Al is sad to go home.

1. Where does Al like to go?
   **the planet Zuru**

2. When does the family visit Zuru?
   **every summer**

3. What animals does the family pet?
   **the red lions**

4. What color are the fruit trees?
   **blue**

5. Where does the family swim?
   **in the orange sea**

6. How does Al feel when he goes home?
   **sad**

7. Is this story real or make-believe?
   **make-believe**

CD-104303 • © Carson-Dellosa       71

---

Reading Fiction

Name _____

Read the story. Answer the questions.

## Libby's Pet Fish

Libby went to the pet store. She wanted to get a pet. Libby looked at the mice. She looked at the hamsters and laughed. She looked at the fish. One fish looked at her and blew a bubble. Libby liked him best. She took him home with her.

1. Where did Libby go?
   **the pet store**

2. What did Libby want to get?
   **a pet**

3. What animals did Libby look at?
   **the mice, hamsters, and fish**

4. Which animals did Libby think were funny?
   **the hamsters**

5. Who blew a bubble at Libby?
   **a fish**

6. Which animal did Libby like best?
   **the fish**

7. What did Libby do with the fish?
   **She took him home with her.**

Reading Fiction

Name _____

Read the story. Answer the questions.

## Tina's Book

Tina has a book about animals. Her father reads her stories from the book. Sometimes her mother reads to her, too. Tina is learning to read. She looks at the pictures. She thinks about the animals. Soon, she will be able to read the stories herself!

1. What does Tina have?
   **a book about animals**

2. What does Tina's father do?
   **reads stories from the book**

3. What does Tina's mother do?
   **reads to her, too**

4. Who is learning to read?
   **Tina**

5. What does Tina look at?
   **the pictures**

6. What does Tina think about?
   **the animals**

7. When will Tina be able to read the stories herself?
   **soon**

Reading Fiction

Name _____

Read the story. Answer the questions.

## Leo

Leo was the king of the lions. He wore a bright crown on his head. His best friend was a mouse named Moe. Moe liked to ride on Leo's back. They walked through the forest every morning. The other animals laughed when they saw a mouse with a lion.

1. Who was Leo?
   **the king of the lions**

2. What did Leo wear on his head?
   **a bright crown**

3. Who was Leo's best friend?
   **a mouse named Moe**

4. What did Moe like to do?
   **ride on Leo's back**

5. When did Leo and Moe walk through the forest?
   **every morning**

6. What did the other animals do when they saw Leo and Moe?
   **laugh**

7. Is this story real or make-believe?
   **make-believe**

Reading Fiction

Name _____

Read the story. Answer the questions.

## The Fair

Ozzy and Anita went to the fair. Their parents said they could ride one ride each. Ozzy rode the Ferris wheel. He pointed at his house from the top. Anita rode the bumper cars. She screamed and laughed when her car hit another one. The fair was fun for both of them!

1. Where did Ozzy and Anita go?
   **the fair**

2. How many rides could each child ride?
   **one**

3. What did Ozzy ride?
   **the Ferris wheel**

4. What did Ozzy point at from the top?
   **his house**

5. Who rode the bumper cars?
   **Anita**

6. Why did Anita scream and laugh?
   **Her car hit another one.**

7. Did Ozzy and Anita have fun?
   **yes**

## Digging Is Fun

Reading Fiction

Name _____

Read the story. Answer the questions.

Angie was a dog. She liked to dig holes in the ground. One day a cat named Gill came to play. Gill saw Angie digging a hole. He thought it looked like fun. Gill asked Angie if he could help. Angie said he could. She thought Gill was funny!

1. Who was Angie?
   **a dog**

2. What did Angie like to do?
   **dig holes in the ground**

3. What did Gill think about digging a hole?
   **He thought it looked like fun.**

4. What did Gill ask Angie?
   **if he could help**

5. What did Angie say?
   **that Gill could help**

6. What did Angie think about Gill?
   **that he was funny**

7. Is this story real or make-believe?
   **make-believe**

76    CD-104303 • © Carson-Dellosa

## The Painting

Reading Fiction

Name _____

Read the story. Answer the questions.

Maddie liked to paint. One day, she painted a clown with a red nose and a white face. The painting made her smile. It made her think about the circus. Maddie decided to give the painting to her teacher. It would help her remember their class trip to the circus.

1. What did Maddie like to do?
   **paint**

2. What did Maddie paint?
   **a clown**

3. What did the clown look like?
   **He had a red nose and a white face.**

4. What did the painting make Maddie do?
   **smile**

5. What did the painting make Maddie think about?
   **the circus**

6. Who did Maddie decide to give the painting to?
   **her teacher**

7. What would the painting help Maddie's teacher remember?
   **their class trip to the circus**

CD-104303 • © Carson-Dellosa    77

## Tigers

Reading Nonfiction

Name _____

Read the story. Answer the questions.

Tigers are very large cats. They live in places like India and China. Tigers are orange with black stripes. They like to eat meat. They have strong jaws and sharp teeth to eat their food. Today, many tigers also live in zoos. You can go see one!

1. What are two places tigers live?
   **India and China**

2. What do tigers look like?
   **orange with black stripes**

3. What do tigers eat?
   **meat**

4. Why do tigers have strong jaws and sharp teeth?
   **to eat their food**

5. Where do many tigers live today?
   **in zoos**

6. Name another animal you could see at a zoo.
   **Answers may vary.**

78    CD-104303 • © Carson-Dellosa

## Butterflies

Reading Nonfiction

Name _____

Read the story. Answer the questions.

Many people like butterflies because they are colorful. Some butterflies may have spots on their wings. They land on flowers and drink from them. Butterflies start out as caterpillars. Caterpillars eat leaves. Later, they grow wings and fly away!

1. Why do many people like butterflies?
   **because they are colorful**

2. What do some butterflies have on their wings?
   **spots**

3. Where do butterflies land?
   **on flowers**

4. How do butterflies start out?
   **as caterpillars**

5. What do caterpillars eat?
   **leaves**

6. Draw your own butterfly.
   **Answers may vary.**

CD-104303 • © Carson-Dellosa    79

## Pecan Trees

Name _____

Read the story. Answer the questions.

Pecan trees can be found in the southern United States. The trees are tall and have green leaves. Pecans are small brown nuts. You can break open a pecan with your fingers. You can eat the nuts alone or make a pie out of them. Some people like to put pecans on their pancakes!

1. Where can you find a pecan tree?
   **in the southern United States**

2. What do pecan trees look like?
   **tall with green leaves**

3. What do pecans look like?
   **small and brown**

4. How can you break open a pecan?
   **with your fingers**

5. Where do some people like to put pecans?
   **on their pancakes**

6. Name another kind of nut.
   **Answers may vary.**

80    CD-104303 • © Carson-Dellosa

## The Moon

Name _____

Read the story. Answer the questions.

The moon travels around the earth every day. We can see the moon at night. Sometimes it looks round like a ball, and sometimes it looks very thin. Some lucky people have visited the moon, but they cannot live there. People cannot breathe on the moon!

1. Where does the moon travel every day?
   **around the earth**

2. When can you see the moon?
   **at night**

3. What does the moon sometimes look like?
   **a round ball or very thin**

4. Who has visited the moon?
   **some lucky people**

5. Why do people not live on the moon?
   **They cannot breathe on the moon.**

6. Draw a picture of the moon.
   **Answers may vary.**

CD-104303 • © Carson-Dellosa    81

## Skunks

Name _____

Read the story. Answer the questions.

Skunks are black and white. They have big, bushy tails. When a skunk is afraid, it makes a bad smell. This smell is hard to wash off. Skunks eat bugs and worms. They also like to eat plants in people's gardens. People do not like this!

1. What colors are skunks?
   **black and white**

2. What does a skunk's tail look like?
   **big and bushy**

3. What happens when a skunk is afraid?
   **It makes a bad smell.**

4. What do skunks eat?
   **bugs and worms**

5. Why do some people not like skunks?
   **They eat plants in people's gardens.**

6. Name another animal you might see in a garden.
   **Answers may vary.**

82    CD-104303 • © Carson-Dellosa

## Glass

Name _____

Read the story. Answer the questions.

Many things are made of glass. You can look through a glass window. You can drink from a glass cup. Be very careful! If glass breaks, it can hurt you. Some people use glass to make art. You could make a necklace with glass beads.

1. What are many things made of?
   **glass**

2. What can you look through?
   **a glass window**

3. What can you drink from?
   **a glass cup**

4. Why should you be careful with glass?
   **If glass breaks, it can hurt you.**

5. What could you make with glass beads?
   **a necklace**

6. Name something else that is made from glass.
   **Answers may vary.**

CD-104303 • © Carson-Dellosa    83

Name _____

Read the story. Answer the questions.

## Games

Some people like to play board games. They roll dice and move game pieces around the board. They may use cards to tell them what to do. The winner is the person who reaches the finish line first.

1. What do some people like to play?

   board games

2. What do they roll?

   the dice

3. What do they move around the board?

   game pieces

4. What might cards tell them?

   what to do

5. Who is the winner?

   the person who reaches the finish line first

6. What game do you like to play?

   Answers may vary.

---

Name _____

Read the story. Answer the questions.

## Shoes

People wear shoes to keep their feet safe. The ground could hurt your feet. You might wear special shoes for running a race. You might wear old shoes to go hiking. Some shoes have laces. Tie them tight so you do not trip!

1. Why do people wear shoes?

   to keep their feet safe

2. What might the ground do to your feet?

   hurt them

3. When might you wear old shoes?

   to go hiking

4. What do some shoes have?

   laces

5. Why should you tie the laces tight?

   so you do not trip

6. Draw a picture of your favorite shoes.

   Answers may vary.

---

Name _____

Read the story. Answer the questions.

## The Beach

The beach has soft sand. Shells are in the sand. Fish swim in the ocean next to the beach. People like to go to the beach with their family and friends. They sit in the sun. They dip their toes into the water.

1. What does the beach have?

   soft sand and shells

2. Where do fish swim?

   in the ocean next to the beach

3. Who do people like to go to the beach with?

   their family and friends

4. Where do they sit?

   in the sun

5. What do people dip their toes into?

   the water

6. Name another place you might go with your family.

   Answers may vary.

---

Name _____

Read the story. Answer the questions.

## Rain

Do you like to watch the rain? Rain helps plants grow. It makes flowers bloom. Your yard may be muddy after it rains. Mud is made when water mixes with dry dirt. Sometimes you can see a colorful rainbow in the sky after it rains.

1. What does the rain do?

   helps the plants grow

2. What happens to flowers after it rains?

   They bloom.

3. What might happen to your yard after it rains?

   It may be muddy.

4. How is mud made?

   when water mixes with dry dirt

5. What might you see in the sky after it rains?

   a colorful rainbow

6. Name another type of weather.

   Answers may vary.

## Feeding the Dog

Name _____

**1. Read the story.**

Luke has a pet dog named Kip. He feeds Kip every morning. He opens the back door and calls Kip. Kip runs to the door. Luke puts food in his bowl. Kip wags his tail and eats.

**2. Read the sentences. Rewrite them in the correct order on the lines below.**

Kip runs to the door.
Luke calls Kip.
Kip wags his tail and eats.
Luke puts food in Kip's bowl.

1. Luke calls Kip.

2. Kip runs to the door.

3. Luke puts food in Kip's bowl.

4. Kip wags his tail and eats.

88    CD-104303 • © Carson-Dellosa

## Cooking Soup

Name _____

**1. Read the story.**

Clay is cooking soup. He puts a large pot on the stove. He opens a can of beans. Then, he opens a can of corn. He puts the food in the pot. Clay heats the soup. It will taste great!

**2. Read the sentences. Rewrite them in the correct order on the lines below.**

He opens the cans.
He heats the soup.
He puts the food in the pot.
He puts a pot on the stove.

1. He puts a pot on the stove.

2. He opens the cans.

3. He puts the food in the pot.

4. He heats the soup.

CD-104303 • © Carson-Dellosa    89

## Washing Clothes

Name _____

**1. Read the story.**

Ned needs to wash his dirty clothes. First, he sorts the colors. The white shirts go together. He puts the clothes in the washer. Then, he puts in the soap. When the clothes are clean, Ned puts them in the dryer.

**2. Read the sentences. Rewrite them in the correct order on the lines below.**

He puts the clothes in the dryer.
He puts the clothes in the washer.
He sorts the colors.
He puts the soap in the washer.

1. He sorts the colors.

2. He puts the clothes in the washer.

3. He puts the soap in the washer.

4. He puts the clothes in the dryer.

90    CD-104303 • © Carson-Dellosa

## The Big Dance

Name _____

**1. Read the story.**

Meg's sister Susan is going to a big dance. Everyone in her class will be there. She is getting ready. She washes her hair. She puts on her dress. She pins a flower on her dress. Mom will drive her to school.

**2. Read the sentences. Rewrite them in the correct order on the lines below.**

She pins on a flower.
She washes her hair.
Mom drives her to the school.
She puts on her new dress.

1. She washes her hair.

2. She puts on her new dress.

3. She pins on a flower.

4. Mom drives her to the school.

CD-104303 • © Carson-Dellosa    91

Name _____

1. Read the story.

### Painting a Room

Dee wanted to paint her room. She and her mom went to the store to buy paint and brushes. They put on old clothes. Then, they rubbed the walls to make them smooth. They dipped the brushes in the paint. They painted the walls. Dee loves her new room!

2. Read the sentences. Rewrite them in the correct order on the lines below.

They put paint on the walls.
They went to the store.
They put on old clothes.
They rubbed the walls.

1. They went to the store.

2. They put on old clothes.

3. They rubbed the walls.

4. They put paint on the walls.

92                    CD-104303 • © Carson-Dellosa

---

Name _____

1. Read the story.

### Emmy's Hamster

Emmy has a pet hamster. She takes good care of him. Every day she cleans his cage. Then, she feeds him grain and seeds. After that, she puts him on her lap and plays with him. She puts him back in his cage. He runs in a wheel. Emmy thinks hamsters are fun pets!

2. Read the sentences. Rewrite them in the correct order on the lines below.

She cleans his cage.
He runs in a wheel.
She feeds him.
She puts him back in his cage.
She plays with him.

1. She cleans his cage.

2. She feeds him.

3. She plays with him.

4. She puts him back in his cage.

5. He runs in a wheel.

CD-104303 • © Carson-Dellosa                    93

---

Name _____

1. Read the story.

### Mailing a Postcard

Derek wanted to send a postcard to his friend Lori. First, he found a card with a picture of a cat. Then, he wrote a note on the card. He put Lori's name and address on it. He stuck a stamp on the card and dropped it in the mailbox. Lori was happy to read the postcard!

2. Read the sentences. Rewrite them in the correct order on the lines below.

Derek wrote Lori's address.
Lori read the card.
Derek found a card.
Derek mailed the card.
Derek wrote a note.

1. Derek found a card.

2. Derek wrote a note.

3. Derek wrote Lori's address.

4. Derek mailed the card.

5. Lori read the card.

94                    CD-104303 • © Carson-Dellosa

---

Name _____

1. Read the story.

### Time for School

Cath is going to school for the first time. Mom tells her it is time to get up. Cath eats breakfast and brushes her teeth. She puts on a new dress. Mom helps her tie her shoes. She hands Cath a sack lunch. Then, she walks Cath to the bus stop.

2. Read the sentences. Rewrite them in the correct order on the lines below.

Mom walks Cath to the bus stop.
Cath puts on a dress.
Cath eats breakfast.
Mom hands Cath a sack lunch.
Mom ties Cath's shoes.

1. Cath eats breakfast.

2. Cath puts on a dress.

3. Mom ties Cath's shoes.

4. Mom hands Cath a sack lunch.

5. Mom walks Cath to the bus stop.

CD-104303 • © Carson-Dellosa                    95

---

Name _____

Sequencing

I. Read the story.

## Bedtime Story

Jon's father reads a story to him each night. Jon brushes his teeth. Then, he gets in bed, and his father sits in a chair. He reads a story and tells Jon good night. Jon dreams about the story.

2. Read the sentences. Rewrite them in the correct order on the lines below.

Jon's father tells him good night.
Jon brushes his teeth.
Jon dreams about the story.
Jon gets in bed.
Jon's father sits in a chair.

1. **Jon brushes his teeth.**

2. **Jon gets in bed.**

3. **Jon's father sits in a chair.**

4. **Jon's father tells him good night.**

5. **Jon dreams about the story.**

96                           CD-104303 • © Carson-Dellosa

---

Name _____

Sequencing

I. Read the story.

## Playing Tag

My friends and I played tag. We picked teams. Mimi was picked first. She is a good player. Rita ran fast in the game. It was hard to catch her. Then, Zeke hid behind a tree. We could not find him. We were tired at the end of the day. It was a fun day.

2. Read the sentences. Rewrite them in the correct order on the lines below.

Zeke hid behind a tree.
Rita ran fast.
We looked for Zeke.
Mimi was picked first.
We were tired.

1. **Mimi was picked first.**

2. **Rita ran fast.**

3. **Zeke hid behind a tree.**

4. **We looked for Zeke.**

5. **We were tired.**

CD-104303 • © Carson-Dellosa                           97

---

Name _____

Sequencing

I. Read the story.

## Fun at the Beach

Abe and Anna went to the beach. They put on their swimsuits. They put sandals on their feet. Abe ran on the soft sand. Anna chased a ball to the sea. The sun was hot, so they got in the water. They splashed each other and laughed.

2. Read the sentences. Rewrite them in the correct order on the lines below.

They splashed and laughed.
They put on their swimsuits.
Abe ran on the sand.
They went to the beach.
They got in the water.

1. **They went to the beach.**

2. **They put on their swimsuits.**

3. **Abe ran on the sand.**

4. **They got in the water.**

5. **They splashed and laughed.**

98                           CD-104303 • © Carson-Dellosa

---

Name _____

Sequencing

I. Read the story.

## Picking a Puppy

Mom said I could get a pet. We went to the store. We looked at some puppies. A black one licked me. Then, a white one wagged its tail. It was hard to choose. We picked the little spotted puppy with the sad eyes. I will take good care of him.

2. Read the sentences. Rewrite them in the correct order on the lines below.

We picked the spotted puppy.
A black one licked me.
We looked at some puppies.
Mom said I could get a pet.
A white one wagged its tail.

1. **Mom said I could get a pet.**

2. **We looked at some puppies.**

3. **A black one licked me.**

4. **A white one wagged its tail.**

5. **We picked the spotted puppy.**

CD-104303 • © Carson-Dellosa                           99

---

Name _____

1. Read the story.

### Our Picnic

Our family went on a picnic in the park. My brother brought a friend. Dad cooked burgers on the grill. I made a salad. Mom served ice cream after we ate. After the ice cream, we played on the swings. Mom and Dad rested under the trees. Then, we went home.

2. Read the sentences. Rewrite them in the correct order on the lines below.

We played on the swings.
We went home.
Dad cooked burgers.
Mom and Dad rested.
Mom served ice cream.

1. **Dad cooked burgers.**

2. **Mom served ice cream.**

3. **We played on the swings.**

4. **Mom and Dad rested.**

5. **We went home.**

100                     CD-104303 • © Carson-Dellosa

---

Name _____

1. Read the story.

### Zak's Sister

Zak has a baby sister. He helps take care of her on Saturdays. In the morning, he brushes her hair. In the afternoon, he makes funny faces so she will laugh. In the evening, he feeds her. Then, he puts her to bed. Finally, Zak goes to bed. Zak's mom says Zak is a good big brother.

2. Read the sentences. Rewrite them in the correct order on the lines below.

Zak goes to bed.
Zak feeds her.
He makes funny faces.
He brushes her hair.
He puts her to bed.

1. **He brushes her hair.**

2. **He makes funny faces.**

3. **Zak feeds her.**

4. **He puts her to bed.**

5. **Zak goes to bed.**

CD-104303 • © Carson-Dellosa                     101

---

Name _____

1. Read the story.

### After School

Erin likes to go to Grandpa's after school. He picks her up at the school gate. They drive to his house. Erin hangs up her coat while Grandpa makes her a snack. She eats the food and then does her homework. Sometimes they watch TV!

2. Read the sentences. Rewrite them in the correct order on the lines below.

Erin does her homework.
Grandpa picks Erin up.
Erin hangs up her coat.
They drive to Grandpa's house.
Erin eats a snack.

1. **Grandpa picks Erin up.**

2. **They drive to Grandpa's house.**

3. **Erin hangs up her coat.**

4. **Erin eats a snack.**

5. **Erin does her homework.**

102                     CD-104303 • © Carson-Dellosa

---

Name _____

1. Read the story.

### Stan's Party

Stan had a party last week. Dad baked a cake. Stan's friends came at noon. First, they played games. Then, they ate cake. After the cake, Stan opened his presents. Everyone had a great time.

2. Read the sentences. Rewrite them in the correct order on the lines below.

Stan opened his presents.
Dad baked a cake.
They ate cake.
They played games.
Stan's friends came.

1. **Dad baked a cake.**

2. **Stan's friends came.**

3. **They played games.**

4. **They ate cake.**

5. **Stan opened his presents.**

CD-104303 • © Carson-Dellosa                     103

# Congratulations!

receives this award for

_____

Signed _____

Date _____

| | | | |
|---|---|---|---|
| afraid | always | angry | aunt |
| balloon | basketball | beautiful | box |
| breakfast | bright | butterfly | cage |
| careful | catch | climb | clock |

© CD

| different | crown | coat | clown |
| fence | elephant | earth | dolphin |
| fold | fly | flower | finger |
| glue | funny | fork | forest |

© CD

| | | |
|---|---|---|
| **great** | **guard** | **hamster** | **honk** |
| **huge** | **jeans** | **joke** | **king** |
| **kitten** | **knife** | **lion** | **leaf** |
| **mail** | **milk** | **morning** | **neat** |

© CD

| necklace | night | ocean | open |
|----------|-------|-------|------|
| © CD | © CD | © CD | © CD |

| pair | parrot | pencil | piece |
|------|--------|--------|-------|
| © CD | © CD | © CD | © CD |

| plant | point | pretty | quick |
|-------|-------|--------|-------|
| © CD | © CD | © CD | © CD |

| return | ring | round | roll |
|--------|------|-------|------|
| © CD | © CD | © CD | © CD |

| | |
|---|---|
| scare | scream |
| shovel | shut |
| squirrel | stove |
| taste | teacher |

| | |
|---|---|
| shell | shark |
| special | snake |
| swing | study |
| thick | thank |

| together | throw | thought | thin |
|----------|-------|---------|------|
| © CD | © CD | © CD | © CD |
| visit | vine | uncle | truck |
| © CD | © CD | © CD | © CD |
| wave | watch | warm | wag |
| © CD | © CD | © CD | © CD |
| young | wood | wide | whisper |
| © CD | © CD | © CD | © CD |